stuart rook
tony charles

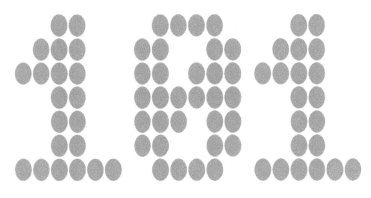

multi-skill
sports games

BLOOMSBURY

LONDON • NEW DELHI • NEW YORK • SYDNEY

Published by Bloomsbury Publishing Plc
50 Bedford Square
London WC1B 3DP
www.bloomsbury.com

First edition 2013

ISBN (print) 978 1 4081 8225 3
ISBN (e-pub) 978 1 4729 0052 4
ISBN (epdf) 978 1 4729 0053 1

Acknowledgements
Cover photograph © Shutterstock
Cover design by Tom Croft and James Watson
Illustrations by Mark Silver
Designed by Margaret Brain
Commissioned by Charlotte Croft
Edited by Sarah Cole

10/12pt DIN Regular by Margaret Brain, Wisbech, Cambridgeshire

Printed and bound in Great Britain by CPI Group (UK) Ltd, Croydon, CR0 4YY
10 9 8 7 6 5 4 3 2 1

CONTENTS

ABOUT FOUNDATION FOOTBALL

Foundation Football is dedicated to improving the quality of coaching to young players. It is one of London's leading independent, award-winning coaching companies, coaching children from Key Stage 1 upwards. We have coached across Europe, North America and Asia with the aim of improving the quality of coaching to boys and girls of all ages and abilities, hopefully laying the foundations for their football futures.

Foundation Football believes all children, whatever their circumstances or level of ability, should be able to participate in and enjoy sport. It can improve a child's confidence, encourage them to get involved with the session, to have and to learn the skills to participate and to show a desire to improve and achieve.

Foundation Football provides children with the opportunity to access sport during the school day and also evenings, weekends and school holidays. We also provide Local Education Authorities with delivery of sessions, tournaments and competitions.

Our enthusiastic coaches give a level of enthusiasm that will meet the energetic needs of every child, delivering sports coaching sessions in primary and secondary schools through fun and informative sessions with fresh ideas. They are all qualified, are always positive role models, show encouragement and provide examples of fair play.

If you require further information about Foundation Football please visit www.foundationfootball.com.

ACKNOWLEDGEMENTS

We would like to thank all of the coaches from Foundation Football for their valuable input, particularly Leon Othen, Craig Lewis and the pupils of Fullwood Primary School, Redbridge.

INTRODUCTION

What are multi-skill sports games?

Multi-skill sports games can be described as activities, games and practices that are designed to challenge participants to learn a range of different skills and techniques that are inclusive, maintain consistent levels of competition, and are challenging – while remaining fun and enjoyable for all participants.

The activities and games in this book aim to introduce and develop specific physical and mental skills to help challenge the physical literacy of young sportspeople through a range of non-sports-specific activities. This is so they can increase their general physical ability before they choose to specialise in any specific sport, while at the same time developing confidence and self-esteem, respect for rules and other people, and the ability to build relationships.

The fundamental principles of multi-skill sports games include:

- Agility
- Balance
- Coordination
- Speed
- Reaction
- Problem-solving
- Observation
- Throwing and catching
- Sending and receiving
- Striking and fielding
- Kicking
- Bouncing
- Movement
- Creating space
- Changing direction
- Skipping
- Running
- Jumping
- Hopping
- Reaction to commands and signals
- Teamwork
- Group games
- Invasion games

These skills and techniques can then be applied to a range of sports and physical activities that the youngster may choose to participate in. Therefore, any session of multi-skill sports games needs to be focused on the development of the basic motor skills that provide a sound base for continued involvement in sport and recreation. This can lead to positive healthy lifestyle choices and other social benefits, while increasing levels of exercise and fitness at a young age.

Who is the book aimed at?

As the sessions included here are non-sports-specific, this book can act as an important resource for sports leaders, coaches and teachers in the sports education sector, local community club volunteers, professional sports coaches, school teachers and midday assistants.

What type of sessions will it help with?

- Curricular PE sessions
- After-school clubs
- Community clubs
- Breakfast clubs
- Lunchtime clubs

In order to help incorporate these games into any curricular PE scheme of learning (particularly for Key Stages 1 and 2) we have included progressions and alternatives for each activity to demonstrate a way of making each session sports-specific. So although multi-skill sports games are non-sports-specific, the activities can be adapted to any session you wish to coach, and to fit the dynamic of any given scheme of learning.

The principles of this book also support the key concepts of Long Term Athlete Development (LTAD) – specifically in the early stages of **Active Start** (basic fitness and movement skills) and **FUNdamentals** (higher focus on aspects such as agility, balance, coordination and speed). Development during this essential stage will enhance performance and increase readiness for the **Learning to Train** phase, and in turn prepare young sportspeople for the higher-level competitive sport phases, **Training to Train** and **Training to Win**, and essentially encourage participants of all ages to pursue a lifetime of physical activity and healthy living – **Active for Life**.

How to use this book

Each session is complemented with a diagram and a description of '**how to set up**' your session, and the '**what you need**' heading gives details of any specific equipment you will need to provide for the players.

The '**how to play**' section gives full details of the rules of the game and provides you with instructions on how to keep a score and/time limit in order to make each game competitive and challenging. Although it is beneficial to keep a score in order to maintain the players' level of engagement, multi-skill sports games generally concentrate more on development, inclusion and the encouragement of fair play – not 'win at all costs'.

Under the '**key skills**' heading you will see some illustrated icons; please see below for more information on what they mean and how to use them to suit your sessions.

'**Progressions and alternatives**' give you extra ideas about how to make the sessions either more or less challenging or age appropriate, and some examples offer a sport-specific alternative.

Learning how to plan a session is one of the most important skills of being an effective sports leader. Knowing the level of ability, age range and level of development of the players you coach will go a long way in knowing what you can coach, what you need to coach, and how you are going to coach it. These factors all come into your plan, and it is essential to know them when developing the players you are coaching. Remember, plan your work, and work your plan!

What do the icons mean?

As part of the description of each game you will see a selection of icons that relate to key skills that each session aims to develop.

These cover a wide range of attributes such as basic physical and mental development to more in-depth decision-making and tactical awareness. The icons are separated into the following six categories:

- Motor skills
- Movement
- Problem-solving
- Teamwork
- Sending and receiving
- Invasion games

Motor skills

The icon above will feature in a large number of the games, as multi-skill sports games and activities are viewed as essential for the development of basic motor skills. These skills include aspects such as **balance**, **agility**, **coordination**, **speed** and **reactions**, and can be challenged in a number of ways.

Examples include using benches during an exercise to test the participant's balance, and tag-based games where the participant has to catch an opponent or pull out a bib to test their agility, coordination and speed.

This icon also symbolises the need for the participant to be able to demonstrate body management and to have increased **spatial awareness** – while both stationary and in motion.

Movement

This icon indicates the development of the player's movement capabilities and basic fitness levels.

It highlights that participants will not only be required to travel from one point to another in any given direction, but also successfully manage multiple **changes of direction**, and will be asked to make **considered movement** with and without an object, such as a ball or a bean bag. During team games and invasion games these movement sessions will aid in developing the ability to **create space** for team mates.

The movement icon encapsulates any game where one player may be following or chasing another, mirroring their actions, and reacting to their movements. It will also include games where the players are collecting and moving objects with different parts of their bodies and different types of physical movement such as **jumping**, **skipping** and **hopping**.

All races and relay practices are included as part of the movement icon and add an extra competitive edge to a number of games.

Problem-solving

This icon is attached to games and activities that are designed to test participants on a mental level, and demands them to develop the ability to find their own solutions to the problems they encounter.

These games will test memory and **observation** skills, require lateral **thinking**, and encourage positive **decision-making**. They will also test a participant's **speed of thought** and **reaction to specific commands and signals** given by the sports leader.

Teamwork

The teamwork icon illustrates the importance of developing the confidence of every participant and the ability to build relationships and work well with others through social interaction.

These group-based games are centred on **inclusion**, **group contribution** and **fair play** through **possession and invasion games**.

Sending and receiving

The throwing and catching icon focuses on **physical dexterity** coupled with **coordination** and the ability to manage a moving object efficiently, such as a ball or a bean bag.

It covers skills such as **throwing and catching** and **striking and fielding**, which can be found in a number of published schemes of learning, and requires the participant to develop the ability to use a variety of sending and receiving techniques using different parts of the body – for example, the action of kicking and controlling/trapping a football with the feet.

Sport-specific sessions and practices will also form part of this icon, wherever a piece of sports equipment is used and a participant is required to use his or her **manipulative skills** to utilise the piece of equipment to successfully strike a object, which could be either moving or stationary – for example, using a hockey stick or a tennis racket to strike a ball.

Invasion games

Following closely on from the teamwork icon, the invasion games icon will offer examples of games and activities where the players aim to develop a deeper understanding of **rules**, **tactics** and **positional sense** during small-sided games.

Invasion games will ask participants to make **specific and considered movement** to **create space** for others, and support team mates in both attacking and defensive situations, while encouraging positive **decision-making** when in possession. Through games, the players will not only learn from one another but also learn through their own mistakes, while simultaneously developing all of the fundamental multi-skills in a competitive but fun environment.

All of the invasion games in this book provide challenging progressions and can be based on team play or small-sided attacking and defending principles in 1 v 1 and 2 v 2 situations.

And finally...

For many young sportspeople, multi-skill sports games will be their primary involvement in any type of physical activity – sports-specific or otherwise. This participation may be with fellow pupils in PE lessons, during time in after-school clubs, or with friends in an extracurricular setting outside of school – such as a youth centre or community club.

We believe that to be a good coach you need to let your personality come across in your sessions. Each page is a guide for you to use: feel free to adapt any game to allow it to work best for you.

In most cases the focus of this participation will be about learning a range of activities and playing the game for fun and enjoyment rather than developing more specific sporting skills. It is important to remember that a high-quality, challenging and progressive multi-skills experience led by a positive and inspiring sports leader is a fantastic starting point for young people on their journey towards lifelong participation in sport.

Finally, our biggest hope is that this book will inspire sports leaders, coaches, teachers, midday assistants and parents to develop fresh, entertaining and informative sessions and that they will always be positive, show encouragement, and provide examples of fair play. Keep up the good work, and keep laying the foundations for the sporting futures of young players.

Happy coaching!

THE SESSIONS

Key

Motor skills

Movement

Problem-solving

Teamwork

Sending and receiving

Invasion games

session 1 target ball

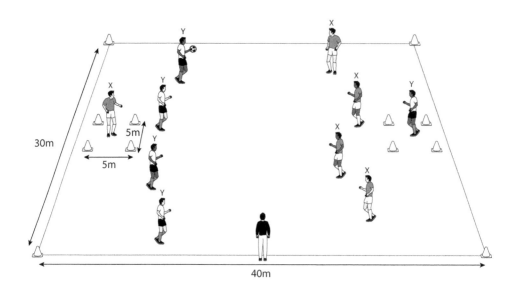

30m

5m

5m

40m

How to set up: Set out a 20 x 30m area with a small square (5 x 5m) in the centre of each end. Arrange players into two small-sided teams (4 v 4 or 5 v 5), with one player in each team standing in the square at the opposite end to their team.

What you need: Bibs, traffic cones, ball.

How to play: Players aim to score a point for their team by throwing the ball to their target player, who is the person standing in the small square. Players are not allowed to move with the ball in their hands and only the target player is allowed in the small square. Once a point is scored, the player who threw the ball becomes the target player.

Key skills

Progressions and alternatives:
1 Limit players to a specific type of pass, such as a bounce pass or only an underarm or overarm throw.
2 Change the size or shape of the ball.
3 The target player may only catch the ball with one hand.

session 2   cat and mouse

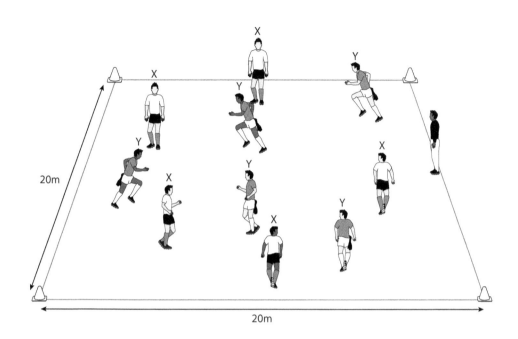

20m

20m

How to set up: Set out a 20 x 20m area. Play 5 v 5 inside the area; one team is 'mice' (Y) and the other 'cats' (X). Each player from the 'mice' team takes a bib and places it into the waistband of their shorts, hanging down like a tail.

What you need: Bibs, traffic cones.

How to play: The cats (X) try to catch the mice (Y) by chasing them around the area trying to pull out their tails. Once the tail is pulled out, both the cat and the mouse are out of the round until all mice are caught. Both teams play as cats, with the sports leader timing both teams to see who is the fastest.

Key skills

Progressions and alternatives:
1 Give both teams a time limit of 30 seconds.
2 Create an 'overload' for the mice. Play six mice v four cats, making it more difficult for the cats.

session 3 capture the flag

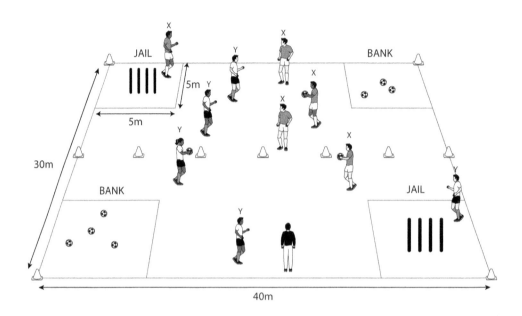

How to set up: Set out a 40 x 30m area. Divide the area into two halves with a centre line of cones. Mark out a 5 x 5m square in each of the four corners of the area. One square in each half is the jail and the other is the bank. Place an equal number of balls of varying shapes and sizes in each team's bank.

What you need: Bibs, traffic cones, balls.

How to play: The aim of the game is to collect all the balls by invading the other team's half of the area, by taking a ball from their bank and carrying it back to your own bank without getting tagged. Players are safe in their own half, but if a player is tagged while in the opponents' half, they must go directly to the opponents' jail. A player is released from jail only when a team mate crosses into the opposing half and high fives them. The first team to collect all of the balls wins.

Key skills

Progressions and alternatives:
1 Allow team members to pass the ball to one another when stealing from the other team.
2 Limit the number of players allowed in the opposition half at any one time.

session 4   bean bag hunt

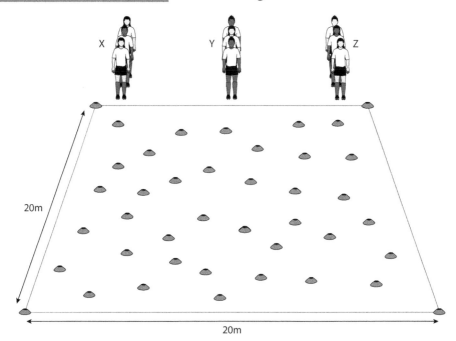

How to set up: Set out a 20 x 20m area with three teams positioned at one end, standing in a line as this game is played as a relay. Place the different-coloured bean bags underneath the cones that are scattered around the area randomly.

What you need: Marker cones, bean bags – 8 of each colour (x 3 colours).

How to play: Players race, one player from each team at a time, to find a bean bag – each of the three teams search for one allocated-colour bean bag (one colour per team). If the player lifts up a cone and it is the correct colour bean bag for their team, they take it back to the starting position. If there is nothing under the cone, or if they reveal a bean bag of a colour of a different team, they leave it there and return empty handed. Players may only look under one cone each time they search. The first team to find the eight bean bags of their allocated colour wins. At the end of the game, the players put the bean bags back under the cones, and then swap places so that for the next round they are searching for a different colour.

Key skills

Progressions and alternatives:
1 Put a time limit on the game, thus encouraging the players to make quick decisions.
2 Allow two players to search at once, working as a pair, or even a whole team at the same time.

session 5 caves

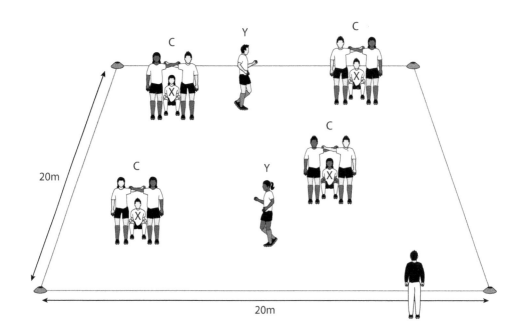

How to set up: Set out a 20 x 20m area.

What you need: Marker cones.

How to play: The sports leader selects two taggers from the group (Y). Arrange the rest of the players into groups of three. Two players join up (C), with their hands on their partner's shoulders, forming an arch to make a cave, while the third player (X) hides from the taggers inside the cave. When the sports leader calls 'go', all players in the cave must move to another cave without getting caught by the taggers. If a player gets tagged, they become the new tagger and all players rotate to make sure every player has a turn at each role.

Key skills

Progressions and alternatives:
1 Increase the number of taggers.
2 Introduce a ball to bounce or dribble with the feet as players move from cave to cave. Taggers then aim to steal the ball.

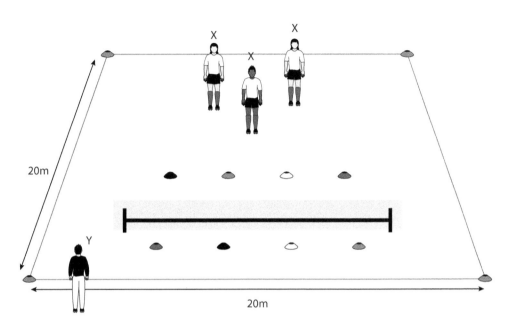

How to set up: Organise players into small groups.

What you need: Marker cones, bench.

How to play: One player is the mastermind (Y) and selects four different-colour cones, but hides this selection from the other players behind a bench (a table or under a cover will work if there are no benches available). The remaining players (X) work as a team and try to guess the correct colour and order by setting out their own cones in a straight line. After each guess the mastermind tells the remaining players if any colours are correct and if they are in the right order. The players aim to guess the correct combination in as few attempts as possible.

Key skills

Progressions and alternatives:
1 Allow players to use a colour more than once in their selection.
2 Allow players to leave a space in their selection.

session 7 foxes and farmers

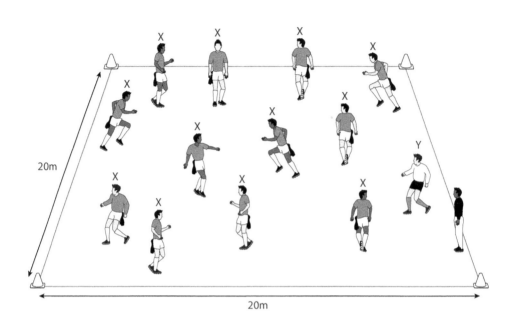

20m

20m

How to set up: Set out a 20 x 20m area. Select one player from the group to be a farmer (Y) while the rest are foxes (X). Each fox takes a bib and places it into the waistband of their shorts, hanging down like a tail.

What you need: Bibs, traffic cones.

How to play: When the sports leader shouts 'go', the farmer chases the foxes around the area and tries to pull the tails off the foxes. If the tail is pulled out, the fox is out of the game, with the last remaining fox being the winner.

Key skills

Progressions and alternatives:
1 Start the game with two farmers.
2 When a fox loses its tail, it becomes a farmer.

session 8   dodgeball

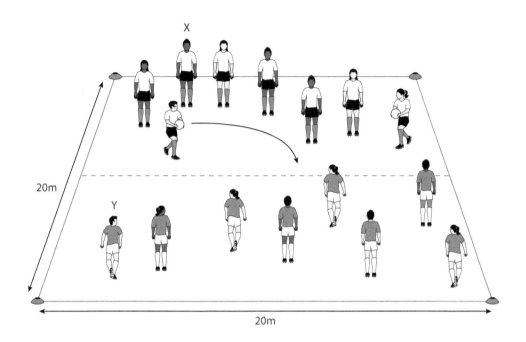

How to set up: Set out a 20 x 20m area with a dividing line across the centre. Organise the players into two teams, with one team standing in each half of the area.

What you need: Bibs, marker cones, soft balls.

How to play: Players throw the soft balls at their opponents from behind their line in order to eliminate them. If a player is hit before the ball bounces, they are out, but if a player catches a ball before it bounces, the player who threw it is out – and a member of their team who has already been eliminated is allowed back in. The game starts with the balls on the centre line and the players race to collect them from the baseline on the sports leader's command. Once all players from one team have been eliminated, the other team has won.

Key skills

Progressions and alternatives:
1 Add more balls, increasing the risk of being hit and eliminated.
2 Use balls of different shapes and sizes.

session 9   lord of the rings

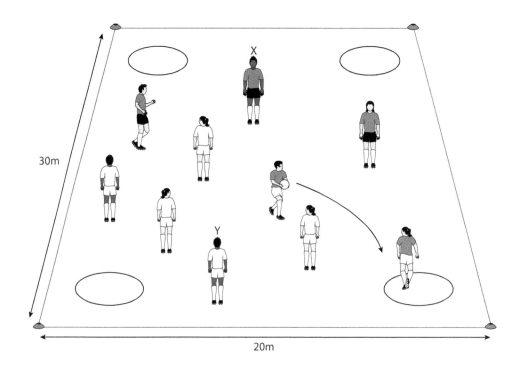

How to set up: Set out a 20 x 30m area with two hoops at each end, one in each corner. Organise the players into two teams, with each team attacking from opposite ends.

What you need: Bibs, marker cones, four hoops, ball.

How to play: Players attempt to score a point for their team by throwing the ball to one of their players who has travelled to, and is standing in, one of the hoops. All players are permitted to move around and may move into the hoops at any point, but players are not allowed to move with the ball in their hands.

Key skills

Progressions and alternatives:
1 Teams can attack hoops that are diagonally across from each other, making the game multi-directional.
2 Limit players to a specific type of pass, such as a bounce pass or only an underarm or overarm throw.
3 Change the size and shape of the ball.

session 10   heads, shoulders, knees and ball

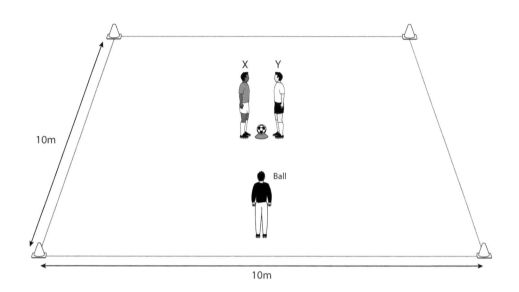

How to set up: Set out a 10 x 10m area. Two players stand opposite each another, with a ball balanced on a cone in between them. Repeat the area for the correct number of players.

What you need: Marker cones, traffic cones, balls.

How to play: As the sports leader calls out a body part, the player has to touch that part of their body. For example, when the sports leader calls 'head', the player touches their head. When the sports leader calls 'ball', the first player to grab the ball is the winner.

Key skills

Progressions and alternatives:
1 Players start with their backs to the ball so they have to turn and grab the ball.
2 Play in groups of three.
3 Use balls of different shapes and sizes.

session 11 four square

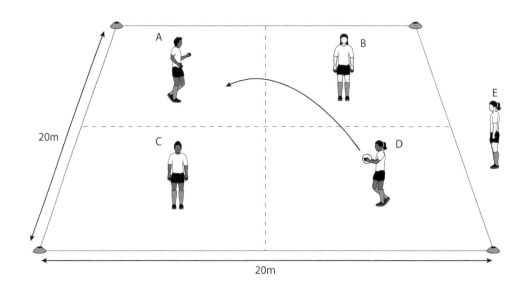

How to set up: Set out a 20 x 20m area which is then divided into four equal 5 x 5m quarters. Repeat the area for the correct number of players. Organise players into groups of five, with one player in each quarter and one waiting by the side.

What you need: Marker cones, large bouncy ball.

How to play: Each player plays as an individual against the other three players, and aims to score points by hitting the bouncy ball into another quarter of the area so that it bounces but cannot be returned. If a player hits the ball out or is unable to return the shot, they swap places with the waiting player (E). A point is scored each time a player makes an error, therefore the aim is to score the fewest amount of points as possible. Set a time limit, and whichever player has the fewest points when the time is up is the winner.

Key skills

Progressions and alternatives:
1 Decrease or increase the amount of playing time.
2 Change the size of the ball.
3 Introduce tennis rackets and balls to make this game sport-specific.

session 12 pairs

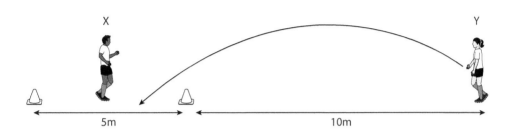

X · 5m · Y · 10m

How to set up: Set out two cones 5m apart from each other in a vertical line. Arrange players into pairs, with one player standing between the two cones and the other standing 5–10m away (age appropriate) with a tennis ball.

What you need: Traffic cones, tennis balls.

How to play: Players aim to score a point for their team by throwing the tennis ball so that it bounces in between the two cones. Their partner scores a point if they catch the ball before it bounces. Keep scores and swap the players around after a given amount of time; the first player to score 10 points wins.

Key skills

Progressions and alternatives:
1 Limit players to a specific type of throw, such as a bounce pass or only an underarm or overarm throw.
2 Change the size or shape of the ball.
3 The catching player may only catch the ball using one hand.

session 13 end to end

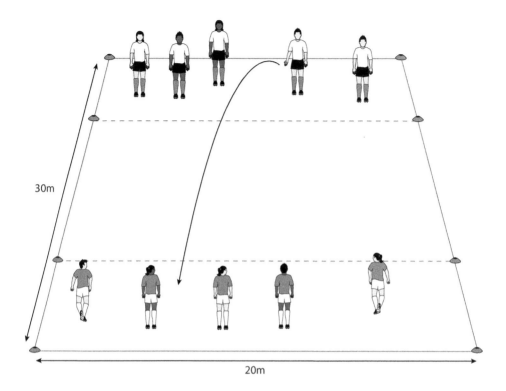

30m

20m

How to set up: Set out a 20 x 30m area with a 5m area marked at each end. Organise the players into two teams and position them in each of the end zones.

What you need: Bibs, marker cones, tennis ball.

How to play: Players attempt to score a point by throwing the tennis ball from their end zone, over the central area so that it bounces in the other team's end zone. If a player touches the ball before it bounces or if the ball bounces in the central area, no point is scored.

Key skills

Progressions and alternatives:
1 Use balls of different shapes and sizes.
2 Allow one player from each team into the other team's end zone to apply pressure to the throwing team. If they catch the ball, they can throw it back to their own team so they can attempt to secure a point.

session 14 dodge it!

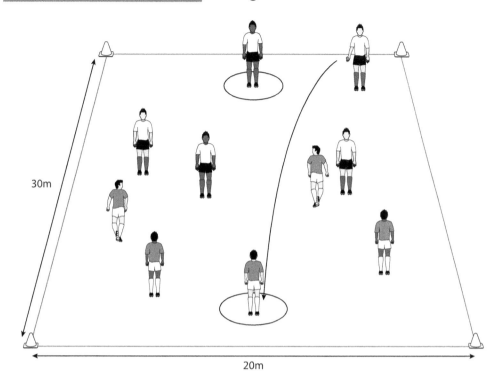

30m

20m

How to set up: Set out a 20 x 30m area with a hoop at each end, in the centre of the area but by the baseline. Organise players into two teams with one player from each team standing in the hoop at their own end.

What you need: Bibs, traffic/marker cones, balls, hoops.

How to play: To score a point, players aim to throw the ball to hit the opposition player in the hoop below the knee. Players may not move with the ball in their hands, therefore encourage teams to work together and pass the ball to gain territory.

Key skills

Progressions and alternatives:
1 Use a larger ball, making it harder for the player in the hoop to dodge the shots, and easier for the outfield players.
2 Use a smaller ball, making it easier for the player in the hoop to dodge the shots, and harder for the outfield players.
3 Change the type of pass to practise different skills, such as a chest pass, overhead throw, bounce pass or underarm throw.

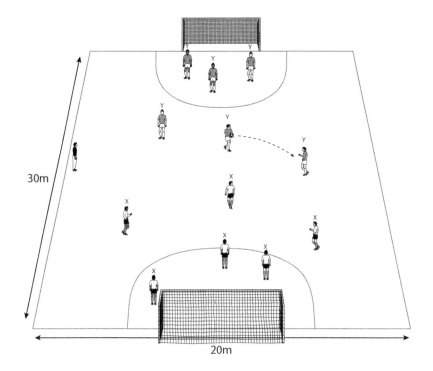

How to set up: Set out a 20 x 30m area, with a goal area marked as a D around the goal at each end. Organise the teams into a 6 v 6 format, with three players in the goal area and three players in the outfield area.

What you need: Bibs, marker cones, ball, large goals or traffic cones.

How to play: Play 3 v 3 in the central area, passing the ball using their hands, with three goalkeepers only allowed in the goal area. Goalkeepers may not use their hands and no outfield player is allowed to move when in possession of the ball. Whenever the sports leader calls 'switch', the three goalkeepers switch places with the three outfield players and the game continues. Players may not move with the ball in their hands. Players score by throwing the ball into the opposition's goal.

Key skills

Progressions and alternatives:
1 Allow goalkeepers to use their hands.
2 Introduce some sports equipment, such as a football to pass or hockey sticks and a ball to pass as a team, or a basketball, and allow players to move with the ball.

session 16 mr ice

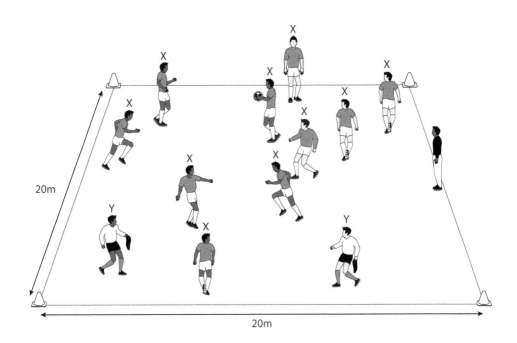

20m

20m

How to set up: Set out a 20 x 20m area.

What you need: Bibs, traffic cones.

How to play: Mr Ice (Y) holds a bib in his or her hand and runs around the area trying to tag the other players (X). Once tagged, the players are frozen and are out of the game and have to stand still exactly where they were caught, becoming obstacles for the players still in the game.

Key skills

Progressions and alternatives:
1 Add another Mr Ice, or Mrs Ice!
2 Add a Mr Fire, who unfreezes the frozen players, allowing them to rejoin the game.
3 Give players different sports equipment to use as they move around, such as a football to dribble, a basketball to bounce, or a hockey stick and a ball to dribble.

session 17 flip it flop it

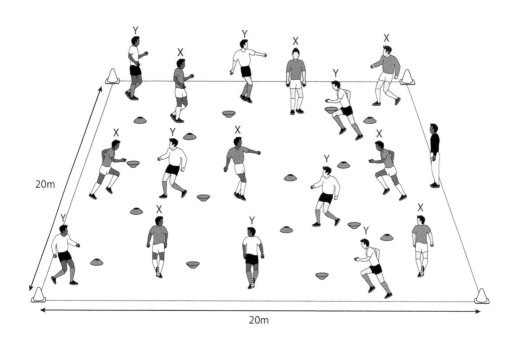

20m

20m

How to set up: Set out a 20 x 20m area and divide the players into two teams. Give each team an equal number of cones and ask one team to set out cones as 'flop it' (right way up, large base to the ground), and ask the other team to set out cones as 'flip it' (wrong way up, small top to ground).

What you need: Bibs, marker cones, traffic cones.

How to play: One group tries to turn the cones over one way – 'flip it' the other the opposite way – 'flop it'. Play for 90 seconds. Whichever team has flipped or flopped the most cones wins!

Key skills

Progressions and alternatives:
1 Reduce the number of cones.
2 Reduce the time limit to make this a quick-reaction activity.
3 Extend the time limit to make this an endurance activity.

session 18 gatecrasher

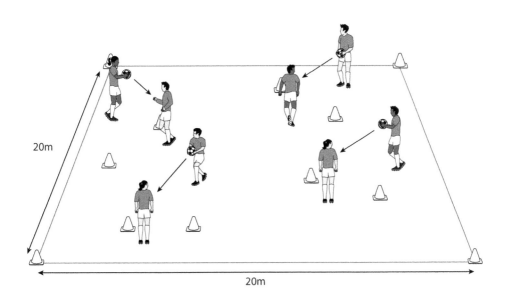

20m

20m

How to set up: Set out a 20 x 20m area. Set out small gates using traffic cones around the area. Players work with a partner and need a soft or bouncy ball – one ball for each pair.

What you need: Bibs, traffic cones, soft or bouncy balls.

How to play: The players work in pairs, moving to each 'gate'. As they arrive at a gate they must make five good passes through it, using their hands and without dropping the ball before moving to another gate. Only one pair can work at a gate at any time.

Key skills

Progressions and alternatives:
1 Vary the type of pass allowed – such as a bounce pass, overhead throw or underarm throw.
2 Change the size or shape of the ball.
3 Introduce a time limit. How many gates can you visit in 60 seconds?
4 Have one pair of defenders in the area without a ball. Defenders try to steal the ball from the other players in the area.

session 19 train ride

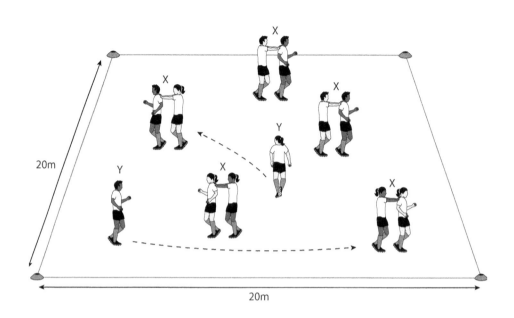

How to set up: Set out a 20 x 20m area.

What you need: Marker cones.

How to play: Players work in pairs (X), with one player standing behind their partner with their hands on their partner's shoulders, both facing forward to create a train. The sports leader also selects two chasers (Y), who move around the area trying to catch a train. If a chaser manages to join on the back of the train, the person at the front of the train is released and now becomes a chaser.

Key skills:

Progressions and alternatives:
1 Start the game with additional chasers.
2 Players work in groups of three to make a longer train.

session 20 cone carnage

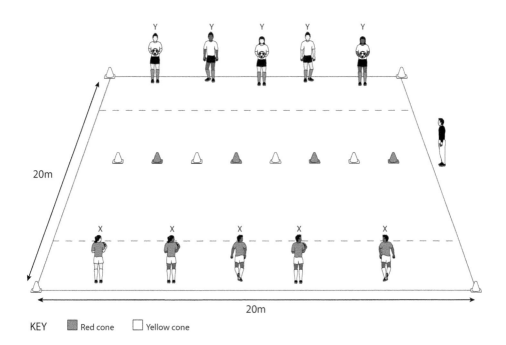

20m

20m

KEY ■ Red cone ☐ Yellow cone

How to set up: Set out a 20 x 20m area, with different-coloured traffic cones lined up across the centre of the area (two colours). Split players into two teams who start at the baseline of each side of the area, facing the cones, with three or four balls per team.

What you need: Bibs, marker cones, balls, traffic cones.

How to play: Players roll or throw the balls, trying to knock down the traffic cones in the centre. For example, X players aim for red cones, Y players aim for yellow cones. Players must stay behind the line when rolling the balls but may move forward to collect another ball. The first team to knock down their allocated-colour cones wins!

Key skills

Progressions and alternatives:
1 Change the type of throw to practise different skills, such as a chest pass, overhead throw, bounce pass, or underarm throw.
2 Increase the distance of the baseline so players have to throw further.
3 Use balls of different shapes and sizes.

session 21 touchdown

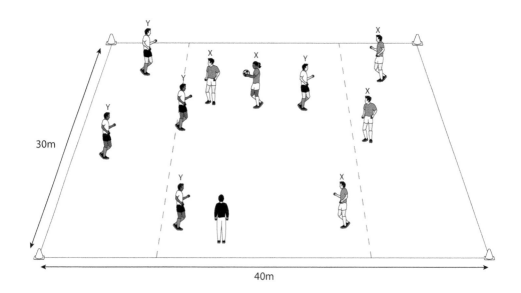

30m

40m

How to set up: Set out a 20 x 30m area, with a touchdown zone at each end 5m from the goal line. Arrange the players into two teams, attacking from opposite ends.

What you need: Bibs, marker cones, ball.

How to play: Players aim to score a point by throwing the ball to a team mate in the other team's end zone and touching it down to the floor, similar to American Football. Players are not allowed to move with the ball in their hands.

Key skills

Progressions and alternatives:
1 Add a permanent defender from each team in the end zone to guard the defensive area.
2 Position a player from each team to stay in the touchdown area only.
3 Change the type of pass to practise different skills, such as a chest pass, overhead throw, bounce pass, or underarm throw.

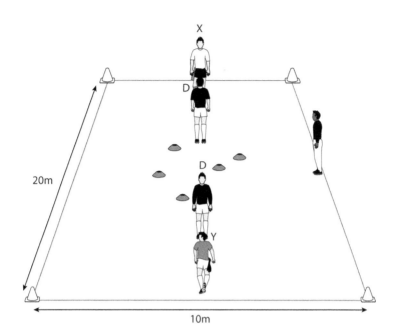

How to set up: Set out a 20 x 10m area with five marker cones scattered in the centre of the area. Players X and Y take a bib each and put it into the waistband of their shorts, hanging down like a tail. Repeat the area for the correct number of players.

What you need: Bibs, marker cones, traffic cones.

How to play: On the sports leader's command, the X and Y players try to steal a cone from the centre of the area. The defenders (D) try to defend the cones, by attempting to pull out the tail of the X or Y player. If the tail is pulled out, the attacking player starts again. Play until all the cones have been collected. Whichever player (X or Y) has the most cones is the winner.

Key skills

Progressions and alternatives:
1 Play with two attackers against one defender, with ten cones scattered in the central area.
2 Play with two attackers against two defenders, with ten cones scattered in the central area.
3 Play with a time limit, with the winner being the player who collects the most cones within the time limit.

session 23 drop it in

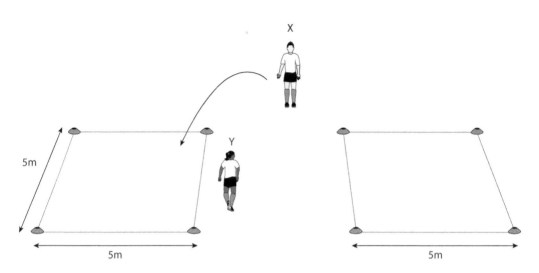

How to set up: Set out two 5 x 5m areas – the two areas need to be next to each other, but 5m apart. Arrange players into pairs, with one player standing in between the two squares and the other player standing 5–10m away (age appropriate) holding a tennis ball.

What you need: Marker cones, tennis ball.

How to play: A player aims to score a point by throwing the ball underarm so that it bounces in one of the two squares. Their opponent must try to defend the two areas and attempt to stop the ball bouncing by either catching it or deflecting it away. Players take ten throws each; whoever has scored the most points wins the game.

Key skills

Progressions and alternatives:
1 Change the type of throw, such as to a bounce pass or overarm throw.
2 Change the size or shape of the ball.
3 If the defending player catches the ball with one hand, they score a point and then change places with the thrower.

session 24 olympic bowling

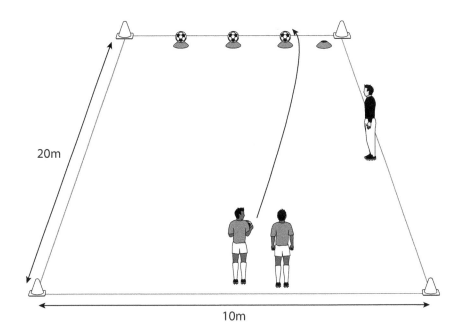

20m

10m

How to set up: Set out a 20 x 10m area. Station two players at one end with a ball. At the other end of the area, balance three balls on three marker cones and have another marker cone spare. Repeat the area for the correct number of players.

What you need: Bibs, marker cones, traffic cones, balls.

How to play: The players work in pairs, taking it in turns to roll the ball and trying to knock a ball at the other end of the area off the marker cone. The player then retrieves the ball for their partner's turn. The first team to knock down their three balls wins the gold medal!

Key skills

Progressions and alternatives:
1 Change the type of throw to practise different skills, such as a chest pass, overhead throw, bounce pass, or underarm throw.
2 Once a ball has been knocked off a cone, the player may take that ball and place it on the spare cone of a different team. The first team to have four empty cones is the winner.

session 25 traffic lights

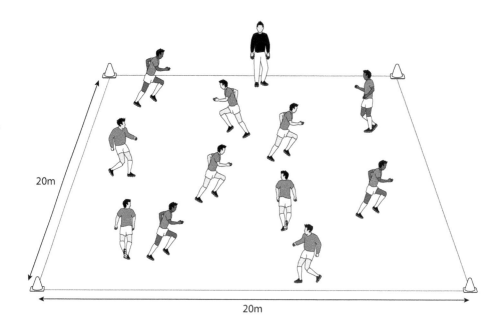

How to set up: Set out a 20 x 20m area.

What you need: Bibs, marker cones, balls.

How to play: Players move around inside the area listening to the sports leader's instructions. Each instruction has a simple movement to follow.

Examples of instructions:
Green Light = Go (move around the area)
Red Light = Stop (stand still)
Yellow Light = Get ready to go (jog on the spot)
Reverse = Move around the area backwards
Speed bump = Lie down on back on the floor (if it's not wet or muddy)

Key skills

Progressions and alternatives:
1 The sports leader makes up more commands.
2 Give players different sports equipment to use as they move around, such as a football to dribble, a basketball to bounce, or a hockey stick and a ball to dribble.

session 26 king of the court

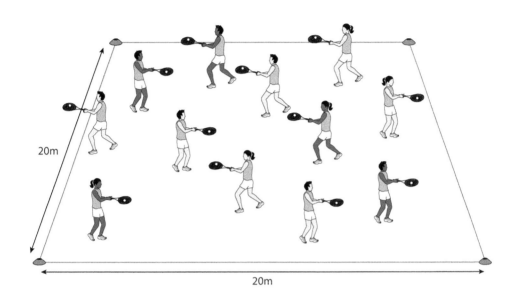

How to set up: Set out a 20 x 20m area. Give each player a tennis racket and a tennis ball and organise them into a space inside the area.

What you need: Marker cones, tennis balls, tennis rackets.

How to play: Players move around the area with their tennis ball balanced on their tennis racket. Players must have two hands on the racket at all times and must always be moving. If the ball falls off the racket at any stage while the player is moving around, they are out of the game – with the last remaining player named king of the court!

Key skills

Progressions and alternatives:
1 Add a 'court jester' who moves around the area trying to put the players off – non-contact.
2 Allow the players to lightly nudge each other if they get close enough to another player to knock them off balance – only light, shoulder-to-shoulder contact is permitted.
3 Only allow the player to use one hand on the racket.

session 27 line kings

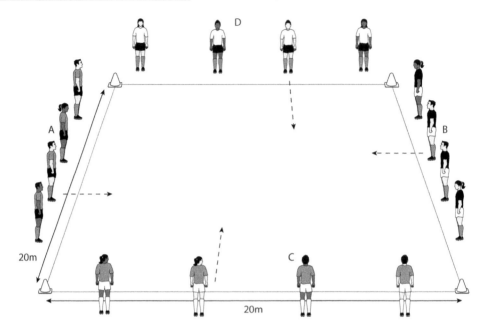

How to set up: Set out a 20 x 20m area with a traffic cone in each corner.

What you need: Bibs, marker cones, traffic cones.

How to play: Players are divided into four teams and stand with one team on the line of each of the four sides of the square. When the sports leader says 'go', the players all move around inside the area, being careful not to bump into one another. When the sports leader calls 'lines', all the players have to touch the nearest traffic cone then return to their original line. The first team with all of its players back on the line wins.

Key skills

Progressions and alternatives:

1 Introduce different types of movement inside the area, such as jumping, hopping, side skips, and running forwards and backwards.
2 Ask players to touch two different traffic cones before returning to their own line.
3 After the call of 'lines', if any two players bump into or touch each other, they must freeze and are out of the game – the team with the most players back on its line wins.
4 Give players different sports equipment to use as they move around, such as a football to dribble, a basketball to bounce, or a hockey stick and a ball to dribble.

session 28 nudge it

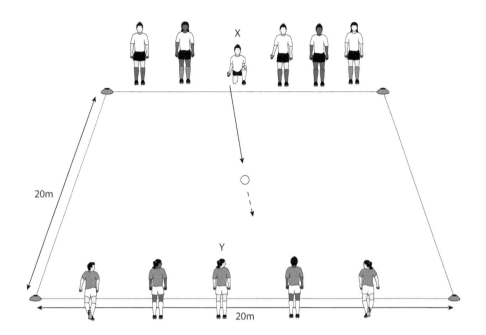

(Game submitted by Foundation Sports coach Craig Lewis)

How to set up: Set out a 20 x 20m area, with one bouncy ball placed in the centre of the area.

What you need: Bibs, marker cones, bouncy ball, tennis balls.

How to play: Arrange the players into two teams and position each team behind each baseline of the area. Players must stay behind their baseline and roll the tennis balls in order to try to hit the larger bouncy ball and nudge it forward towards the other team's baseline. The first team to nudge the bouncy ball past the other team's baseline wins the game.

Key skills

Progressions and alternatives:
1 Change the type of pass to practise different skills, such as a chest pass, overhead throw, bounce pass, or underarm throw.
2 Decrease the number of tennis balls.
3 Increase the distance of the baselines to make the roll/throw further.

session 29 around the clock

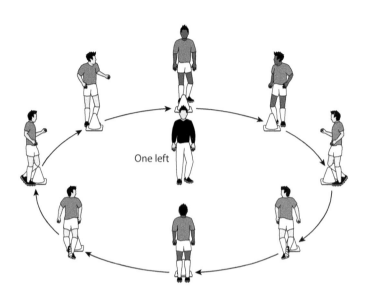

One left

How to set up: Set out a circle with traffic cones; the size will depend on the number of players. One player stands behind each cone.

What you need: Traffic cones, balls.

How to play: The sports leader calls out a series of commands which relate to movements, making them more and more difficult each time. For example, one left = move to the cone to your left; one left, one centre, two right = one to the left, in and out of the centre, then two right.

Key skills

Progressions and alternatives:
1 Introduce more complicated combinations.
2 Introduce different movements – forwards, sideways, backwards, etc.
3 Give players different sports equipment to use as they move around, such as a football to dribble, a basketball to bounce, or a hockey stick and a ball to dribble.

bench ball

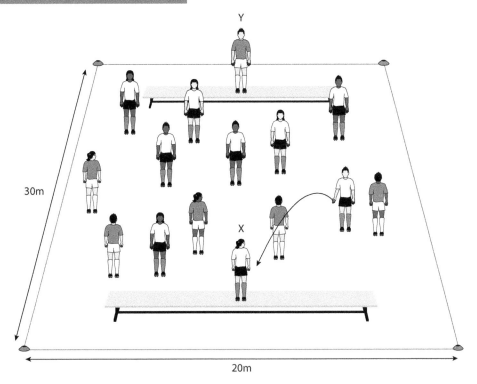

How to set up: Set out a 20 x 30m area with a bench positioned at either end of the area. Arrange the players into two teams with one player standing on the bench at the opposite end to their team.

What you need: Bibs, marker cones, ball, two benches.

How to play: The aim is for players to throw the ball to their bench player to catch. Once the ball is caught, the thrower joins the other player on the bench. The bench player is allowed to move along the bench but not allowed to step off it. Players are not allowed to move with the ball in their hands. The first team to have all of their players standing on the bench are the winners.

Key skills

Progressions and alternatives:
1 Change the type of pass to practise different skills, such as a chest pass, overhead throw, bounce pass, or underarm throw.
2 Use a different size or shape ball.
3 Allow one defender to stand on the bench to try to defend.

session 31 through the zones

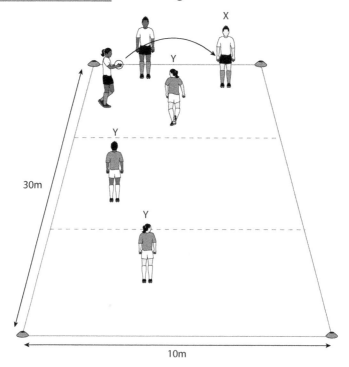

How to set up: Set out a 30 x 10m area, and divide it into three equal zones. Arrange the teams into 3 v 3, with the attacking team all positioned in one zone of the area, but with the defenders spread out with one player in each zone.

What you need: Bibs, marker cones, ball.

How to play: The attacking team plays 3 v 1 in each zone of the area, trying to make ten successful passes. Each time they make ten passes, they score one point and move into the next zone to play against the next defender. The objective is to move through the three zones without dropping or losing possession of the ball. If the ball is dropped or intercepted, the teams swap places and roles, and if a team successfully travels through the three zones, the teams swap roles. Play for a given amount of time, with the winners being the team with the most points.

Key skills

Progressions and alternatives:
1 Change the type of throw, such as to an overarm throw, underarm throw, or a bounce pass.
2 Change the type, size or shape of the ball.
3 Once a team passes into the next zone, the defender may also move across – making the second zone a 3 v 2, then the final zone a 3 v 3.

session 32 roller goal

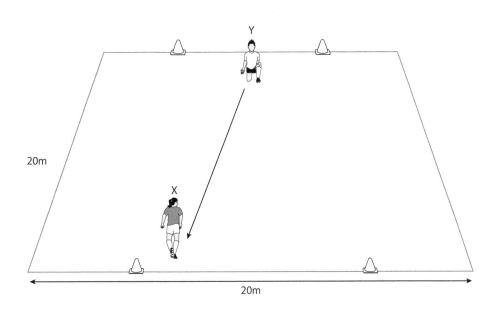

How to set up: Set out two 20 x 20m areas with two 5 x 5m goal areas at each end in the corners. Organise the players into pairs, with one ball per game. Repeat for the correct number of players.

What you need: Bibs, marker cones, traffic cones, tennis ball.

How to play: Players aim to score a point against their opponent by rolling the ball along the floor through either of the two goals at the other end. Players may use any part of their body to stop the ball. The first player to 10 points wins the game.

Key skills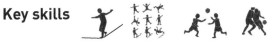

Progressions and alternatives:
1 Change the size or shape of the ball.
2 Only allow players to defend the goals using their feet.
3 Allow players to throw the ball as a bounce pass to try to score; defenders must not use their hands.

session 33   hockey target game

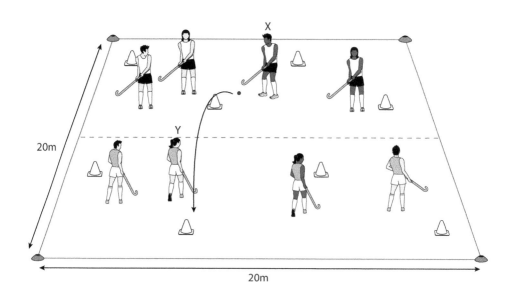

(Game submitted by pupils at Fullwood Primary School, Redbridge)

How to set up: Set out a 20 x 20m area with a dividing line across the centre. In each half place four traffic cones spaced out with two at the front and two at the back. Arrange the players into two teams of four and place them in each half of the area.

What you need: Bibs, marker cones, traffic cones, hockey sticks, small ball.

How to play: Using the hockey stick to hit the ball, the players aim to knock down the cones in the other team's half. If they knock a cone down, it is removed from the area and the players then must aim for the remaining cones. Players must stay in their own half, and the first team to knock down all four cones wins.

Key skills

Progressions and alternatives:
1 Change the position of the cones.
2 Add another ball.
3 Teams must make three passes on their side of the area before attempting a shot at a cone.

session 34 scarecrows

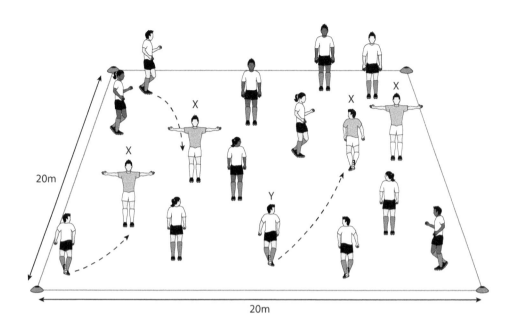

20m

20m

How to set up: Set out a 20 x 20m area.

What you need: Bibs, marker cones.

How to play: Select one or two players to be the taggers, who try to tag the other players as they move around the area, trying not to get caught. When a player gets tagged they have to stand still with their arms out like a scarecrow (Y), but if another player runs underneath their arms they are back in the game. After a minute, change the taggers.

Key skills

Progressions and alternatives:
1 Increase the size of the area to make it more difficult for the taggers.
2 Increase the number of taggers per game.

session 35 rob the nest

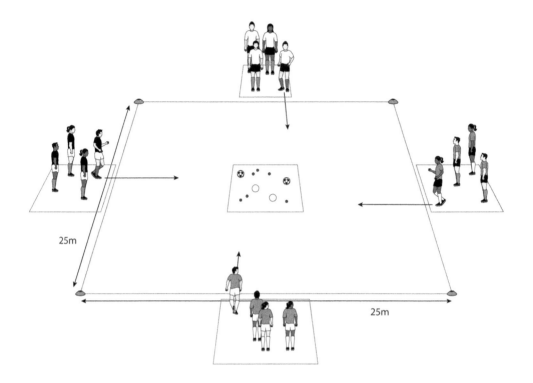

How to set up: Set out a 25 x 25m area, with a 5 x 5m square in the centre of it. On each touchline mark out four 5 x 5m squares. Place as many balls as you can find in the centre square and put the players into four teams in each of the outside squares.

What you need: Bibs, marker cones, lots of balls – different shapes and sizes.

How to play: Like a relay race, when the sports leader shouts 'go', the first member of each team runs out of their square, takes one ball from the centre and returns, and then a team mate can go and rob the nest. The team that collects the most balls after the allocated amount of time wins.

Key skills

Progressions and alternatives:
1 Once all the balls are collected from the centre, allow players to steal a ball from someone else's square; players must go through the middle square on the way there and the way back.
2 Allow players to go two at a time.

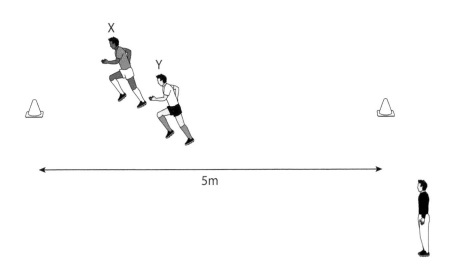

How to set up: Set up two cones 5m apart. Players stand facing each other, in between the two cones. Repeat the area for the correct number of players.

What you need: Traffic cones, one ball between two.

How to play: One player (X) leads, the other (Y) copies. The lead player has to touch a cone to the left or right before the copier (mirror) gets there by trying to outwit their opponent using a 'fake'. Once a cone is touched with the hand, that player gets a point and the players switch roles.

Key skills

Progressions and alternatives:
1 Use a 'double fake' to lose your opponent.
2 Give one of the players sports equipment to use as they move around, such as a football to dribble, a basketball to bounce, or a hockey stick and a ball to dribble.

session 37 nutmeg challenge

How to set up: Organise the players into groups of 5–10, standing in a circle. Players need to stand with their legs apart but with the outside of their feet touching so that the circle is closed.

What you need: Ball.

How to play: The sports leader drops the ball into the circle from above, and the players then attempt to use their hands to push the ball through any other player's legs and out of the circle. As the ball goes through the player's legs, they are eliminated and the circle gets smaller. When the game is down to four players, it becomes sudden death to determine a winner – with the first player to push the ball under another player's legs being the winner.

Key skills

Progressions and alternatives:
1 Only allow the players to use one hand.
2 Change the size or shape of the ball.

session 38 quidditch

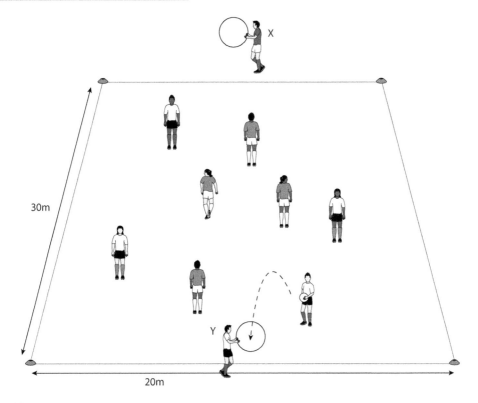

How to set up: Set out a 20 x 30m area with one player holding a hoop at each end. Arrange players into two small-sided teams (4 v 4 or 5 v 5).

What you need: Bibs, marker cones, hoops, ball.

How to play: Players attempt to score points for their team by throwing the ball through the hoop that their end player is holding. The end player must remain static but can move the hoop around above them or from side to side to help their team mates. The ball must travel through the hoop without touching it. Players are not allowed to move with the ball in their hands, and the opposing team may only win possession through intercepting passes. If any player has the ball in two hands nobody is allowed to tackle them.

Key skills

Progressions and alternatives:
1 Play with two hoops at either end to create more attacking opportunities.
2 Limit players to a specific type of pass, such as a bounce pass, or an underarm or overarm throw.
3 Change the size and shape of the ball.

session 39 hand tennis

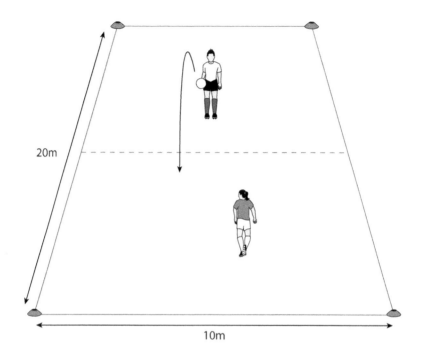

20m

10m

How to set up: Mark out a 20 x10m area with a dividing line across the middle of it. Repeat the area for the correct number of players.

What you need: Marker cones, large bouncy ball.

How to play: This game is played with one player standing in each half of the area. Using only the palm of the hand, each player attempts to hit the bouncy ball into the opponent's half without it bouncing in their own half first. If the ball bounces twice in the opponent's half, they score a point, but if the first bounce is outside the area, the opponent gets a point. Scores can be kept with a singular point being scored or can follow the regular tennis scoring system.

Key skills

Progressions and alternatives:
1 Only allow one bounce.
2 Change the size of the ball.
3 Introduce another player on each side for a game of doubles.

session 40 coconut shy

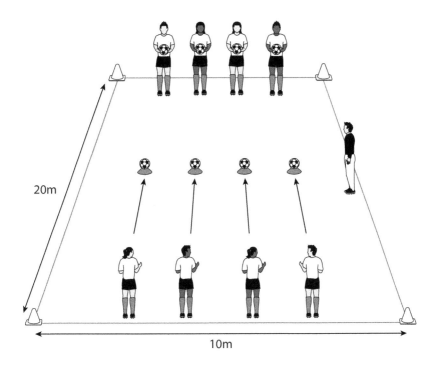

20m

10m

How to set up: Set out a 20 x 10m area. The players work in pairs on opposite sides of the area. In the middle of the area, in between each pair, place a marker cone with a ball balanced on top. Then give out one additional ball to each pair. Repeat the area for the correct number of players.

What you need: Bibs, marker cones, traffic cones, balls.

How to play: The players use their hands to roll the ball across the area with the aim of knocking the ball off the cone in the centre. Each player takes turns with their partner, with one point being scored for each time they knock the ball off the cone.

Key skills

Progressions and alternatives:
1 Change the type of throw to practise different skills, such as a chest pass, overhead throw, bounce pass, or underarm throw.
2 Each time the player knocks the ball off the cone, they take a big step backwards to increase the distance of the pass.
3 Players work in pairs and combine their scores. The first team to 10 points wins.

session 41 ball of life

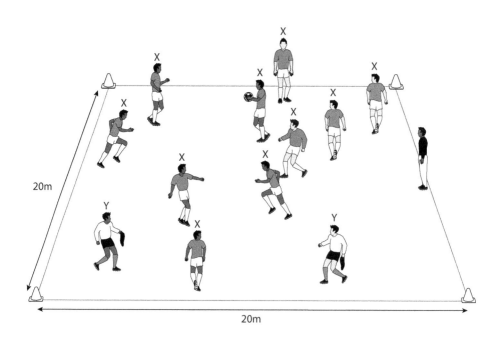

20m

20m

How to set up: Set out a 20 x 20m area.

What you need: Bibs, marker cones, ball.

How to play: The Y players start the game with a bib each, held in their hands. They have to try to tag an X player. If an X player is tagged, they take the bib and change places with the Y player to become the 'tagger'. The X players have one ball between them and may pass the ball to each other using their hands. The player who has the ball in their hands is safe and cannot be tagged.

Key skills

Progressions and alternatives:
1 Add another Y player.
2 Limit the amount of time any player can hold the ball to 5 seconds.
3 Use different passing techniques for the X players, such as a bounce pass, or rolling the ball on the floor.
4 Introduce more balls to the game.
5 Change the size and shape of the balls to tennis balls or rugby balls.

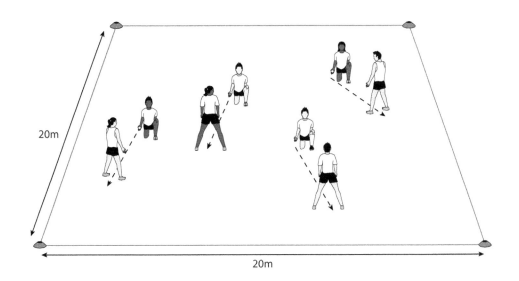

How to set up: Set out a 20 x 20m area. Arrange players into pairs.

What you need: Marker cones, balls, sports equipment.

How to play: Player one holds the ball while player two stands in a space with their legs apart. Player one aims to roll the ball through player two's legs. If it is successful, player one scores a point and player two retrieves the ball, and player one finds a different space. Players continue to take it in turns. The first player to score 5 points is the winner.

Key skills

Progressions and alternatives:
1 Players to use their feet to dribble and pass through the legs.
2 Introduce hockey sticks and balls; players then dribble and pass using the hockey sticks.

session 43 catch-tail

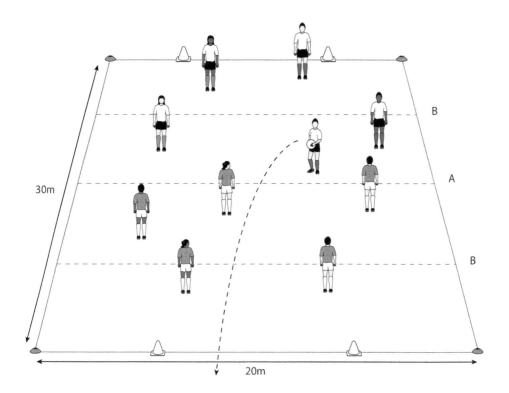

30m

20m

How to set up: Set out a 20 x 30m area, with a wide goal at each end. Divide the area up into four equal sections. Organise players into two teams, with one team standing in each half of the area.

What you need: Bibs, marker cones, ball, goals or traffic cones.

How to play: Players attempt to score points by throwing the ball into the opposition's goal, with 1 point being awarded from behind the halfway line (A) and 3 points from behind the line closest to the goal (B). A point is also awarded if any player on the defending team catches the ball before it bounces. Players must stay in their own half and the first team to score 10 points wins!

Key skills

Progressions and alternatives:
1 Use balls of different shapes and sizes.
2 Ask teams to make at least three passes before they can attempt a throw at goal.

session 44 gladiators

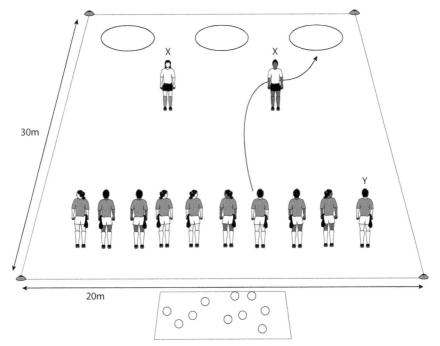

How to set up: Set out a 20 x 30m area with three hoops as target areas at one end and a 'bank' – 5 x 5m square – at the other. Select two players to be the 'gladiators' (X) and give every other player a bib to put into the waistband of their shorts so that it hangs down like a tail, and place an assortment of balls into the 'bank'.

What you need: Bibs, marker cones, hoops, a selection of balls.

How to play: Each player takes a ball from the bank and attempts to run past the gladiators (X) and place it into the target area without getting tagged – having their 'tail' pulled out. If any player gets tagged, they take their ball and return to the start, replace their bib, and try again. Play to a time limit or until all the balls have been placed into the target areas, then change the gladiators.

Key skills

Progressions and alternatives:
1 Increase the number of gladiators.
2 If a player is tagged they are out of the game – if all players are eliminated, the gladiators win; if all the balls are placed in the target areas, the players win.
3 Give each player a tennis racket; they now have to balance the ball on the racket as they travel to the target area. If the ball falls off or if they are tagged, they must return to the start.

session 45 hot shot

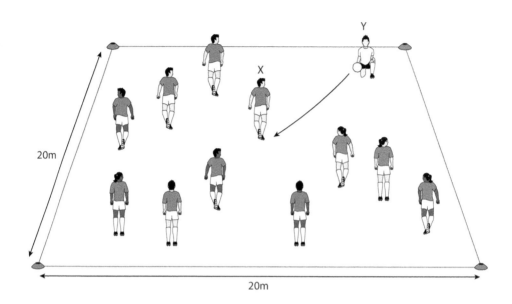

20m

20m

How to set up: Set out a 20 x 20m area. One player (Y) starts with a ball, and the remaining players are spread out inside the area without a ball.

What you need: Bibs, marker cones, soft balls.

How to play: The Y player carries the ball around the area and attempts to hit the X players by rolling the ball, aiming below the knee. Once the X player is hit, they get a ball and join the Y player.

Key skills

Progressions and alternatives:
1 Start the game with two or more Y players.
2 Have one ball between two Y players so they pass to each other, trying to strike out the X players.

session 46 remote control

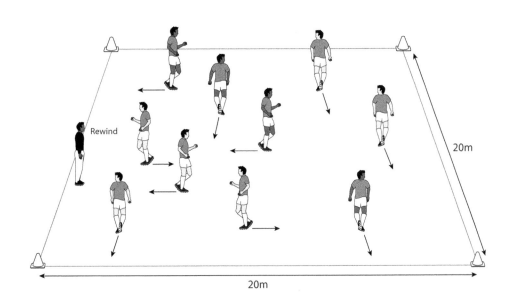

Rewind

20m

20m

How to set up: Set out a 20 x 20m area.

What you need: Bibs, marker cones.

How to play: The players move around inside the area. As the sports leader 'watches TV' and changes the channel using a remote control, the players follow the instructions. Each instruction has a simple movement to follow.

Examples of instructions:
Fast forward = Players move quickly around the area
Slow motion = Players move in slow motion
Rewind = Players move backwards
Formula One = Players pretend to drive around the area in a racing car
Wimbledon = Players pretend to play a tennis match
Grand National = Players pretend to be part of a horse race

Key skills

Progressions and alternatives:
1 The sports leader makes up more commands.
2 Give players different sports equipment to use as they move around, such as a football to dribble, a basketball to bounce, or a hockey stick and a ball to dribble.

session 47 3 v 1 target ball

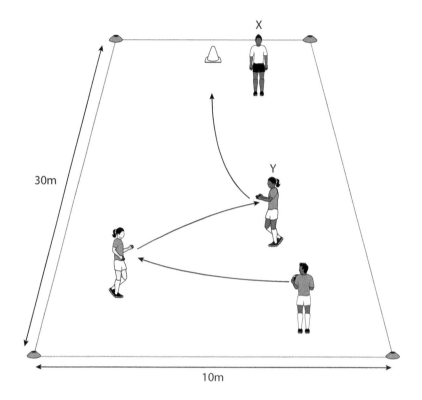

How to set up: Set out a 20 x 10m area with one traffic cone standing at the end of the area. Position three players outside the rectangle and one player inside it.

What you need: Bibs, marker cones, traffic cone, ball.

How to play: The three attackers aim to pass the ball and work as a team to try to knock down the target cone at the end of the area. If the defender successfully intercepts or defends the target cone, they swap places with one of the attackers and the practice restarts. No player may move with the ball in their hands.

Key skills

Progressions and alternatives:
1 Introduce an area that the attacking players must stay out of, so that the throw at the target cone is from a greater distance.
2 Add more defenders to make the practice 3 v 2 and eventually 3 v 3, attacking and defending once possession changes hands.
3 Change the type of pass to practise different skills, such as a chest pass, overhead throw, bounce pass, or underarm throw.

session 48 olympic warm-up

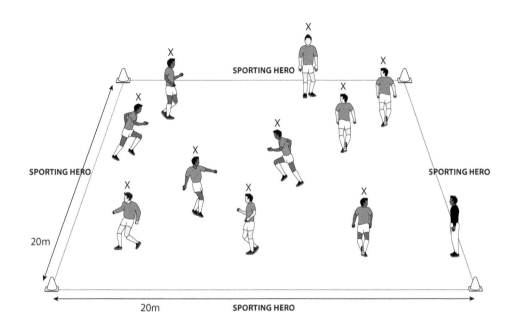

How to set up: Set out a 20 x 20m area and name each side of the area after a famous Olympic hero.

What you need: Bibs, marker cones.

How to play: The players move around inside the area. When the sports leader calls the name of the Olympic hero, all the players run to that line as fast as they can.

Key skills

Progressions and alternatives:
1 Change movements to forward/backwards, side to side, skipping.
2 The last player to arrive at the line is out of the game or does a fun forfeit.
3 Give players different sports equipment to use as they move around, such as a football to dribble, a basketball to bounce, or a hockey stick and a ball to dribble.

session 49 triangle tag

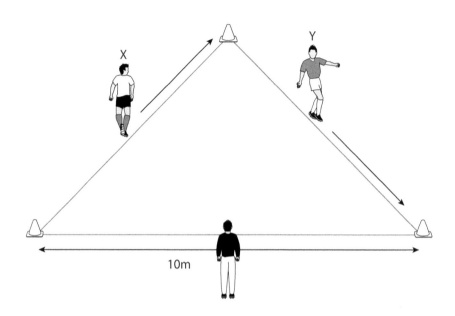

How to set up: Set out a triangle with each point 10m apart. Position two players on the outside of the triangle; one player takes a bib and places it into the waistband of their shorts so that it hangs down like a tail. Repeat the area for the correct number of players.

What you need: Bibs, marker cones.

How to play: Player X tries to tag player Y by chasing them around the outside of the triangle. Player X can move in either direction in order to catch their opponent.

Key skills

Progressions and alternatives:

1 Give players different sports equipment to use as they move around, such as a football to dribble, a basketball to bounce, or a hockey stick and a ball to dribble.
2 Make the triangle larger or smaller to make the game harder or easier.

session 50 cone grabber

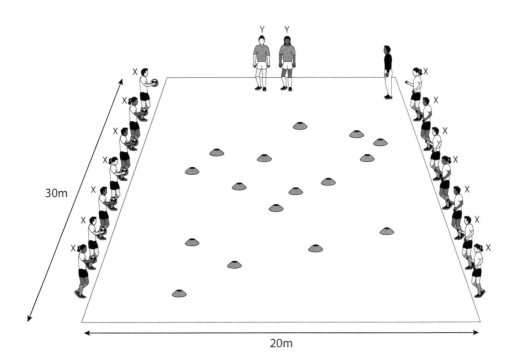

30m

20m

How to set up: Set out a 20 x 30m area. Players work in pairs. Station two players at the start point on the end-line, with the remaining pairs of players facing each other on the sidelines, opposite their partner. Scatter cones randomly across the middle of the area.

What you need: Bibs, marker cones, balls.

How to play: The Y players must run out into the area without being hit on or below the knee by the balls that are being rolled back and forth by the X players. Y players take it in turns to attempt to grab as many cones as they can, but if they get hit, they return to the start point with nothing. Count the number of cones picked up in a 30-second period, then rotate pairs.

Key skills

Progressions and alternatives:
1 Change the type of throw to practise different skills, such as a chest pass, overhead throw, bounce pass, or underarm throw.
2 Reduce the time limit to 20 seconds.

session 51 take three

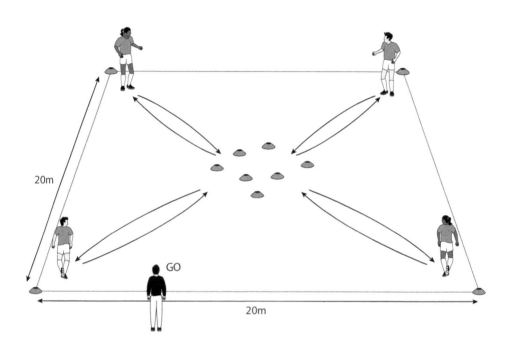

How to set up: Set out a 20 x 20m area, with one player in each corner and seven marker cones in the middle of the square. Repeat the area for the correct number of players.

What you need: Marker cones.

How to play: When the sports leader shouts 'go', the four players race to collect the cones from the centre of the square and return them to their corner. Once the cones have all gone from the middle they may steal cones from each other's corners. The first player to collect three cones is the winner.

Key skills

Progressions and alternatives:
1 Use nine cones. The first to collect four is the winner.
2 Replace cones with footballs/rugby balls/tennis balls.
3 Play in pairs, taking it in turns to collect a cone/ball.

protect the king

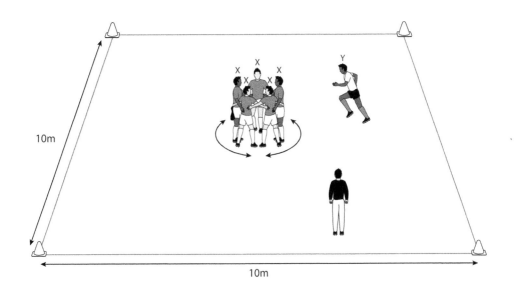

How to set up: Set out a 10 x 10m area. Organise the X players into a circle, facing inwards with arms linked so that they are huddled together. One player is named as the king and places a bib into the waistband of their shorts, hanging down like a tail. Repeat the area for the correct number of players.

What you need: Bibs, traffic cones, balls.

How to play: The huddled-together X players have to protect their 'king' player from having the bib pulled out by the Y player by moving clockwise and anti-clockwise.

Key skills

Progressions and alternatives:
1 Add more X players to make a bigger circle.
2 The Y player dribbles a ball with their feet or bounces a ball using their hands as they move.

session 53 king of the ring

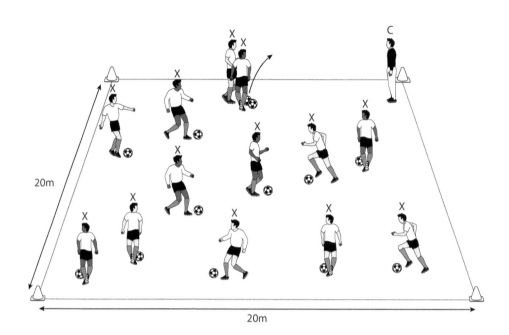

20m

20m

How to set up: Set out a 20 x 20m area. All players have a piece of sports equipment to use – depending on the theme of the session, such as a football to dribble, a basketball to bounce, or a hockey stick and a ball to dribble.

What you need: Bibs, marker cones, sports equipment.

How to play: Players move around the area, trying to avoid all other players. If another player loses control of their ball or gets close enough to an opponent, they can make a tackle and knock the ball out of the area. If a player's ball leaves the area they are out of the game. The last remaining player is the winner.

Key skills

Progressions and alternatives:
1 Start the game with one extra defender, so that now players are on the lookout for the other players and the added defender.
2 Players become defenders once their ball is out of the area.

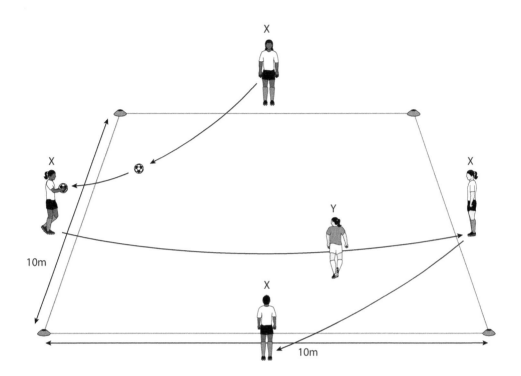

How to set up: Set out a 10 x 10m area with one player standing on each side of the square and one player in the middle. Give the players on the outside a ball.

What you need: Bibs, marker cones, ball.

How to play: The players on the outside of the area aim to make as many passes as they can without the player in the middle intercepting the ball. If the outside players make ten successful passes they choose a forfeit for the player in the middle to do ten times – i.e. star jumps. If the player in the middle intercepts the ball before ten passes, the players on the outside have to do the forfeit to that number – i.e eight passes = eight star jumps. Rotate the players.

Key skills

Progressions and alternatives:
1 Change the type of throw, such as to a bounce pass or overarm throw.
2 Change the size or shape of the ball.
3 Increase the minimum amount of passes to 20.
4 Limit players to only using their feet to pass the ball, or to use hockey sticks and a smaller ball.

session 55 spread your wings

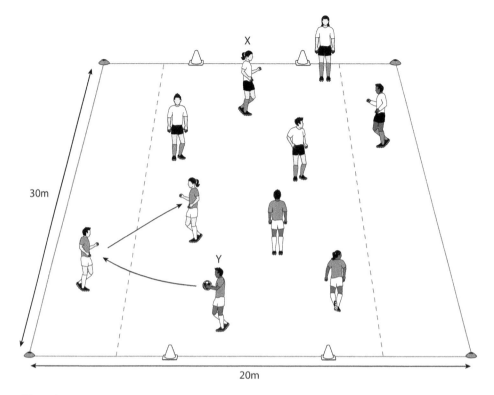

How to set up: Set out a 20 x 30m area with two areas on either side, 10m in from the touchline and with a goal at either end. Position one player for the X team on one side, and one player from the Y team on the other.

What you need: Bibs, marker cones, traffic cones, ball.

How to play: Teams try to score against the opponent by using the wide zones. Use one player in the channel who must touch the ball at least once before the side can score. Players cannot score from the wing, but must pass the ball back into the field of play for someone else to score by throwing the ball into the goal. Players pass the ball using their hands but are not permitted to move with the ball in their hands.

Key skills

Progressions and alternatives:
1 Have a neutral player in the zone; this player is on both teams.
2 Allow one defender into the channel.
3 Change the type of pass to practise different skills, such as a chest pass, overhead throw, bounce pass or underarm throw.

session 56 | skid ball

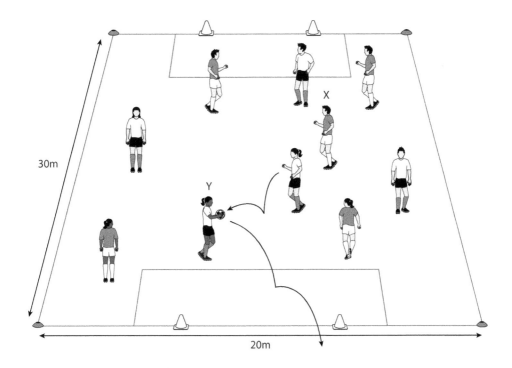

How to set up: Set out a 20 x 30m area with a goal at each end and an area in front of each goal. Arrange players into two small-sided teams (4 v 4 or 5 v 5).

What you need: Bibs, marker cones, traffic cones or mini goals, ball.

How to play: Players attempt to score points for their team by throwing the ball into the goal, but the ball must bounce in the small area before going in. No one is permitted to enter the small area at either end and players may only pass the ball to each other with a bounce pass. Players are not allowed to move with the ball in their hands.

Key skills

Progressions and alternatives:
1 Allow one defender to stand in the small area to act as a goalkeeper.
2 Change the size and shape of the ball.

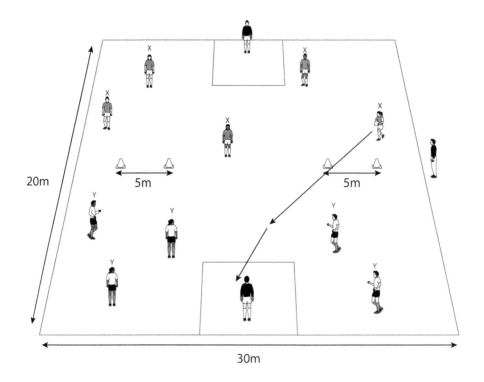

20m

5m

5m

30m

How to set up: Set out a 20 x 30m area with a 5 x 5m square at each end, and two small gates in the middle of the area. Organise the players into two teams.

What you need: Bibs, marker cones, traffic cones, balls.

How to play: The teams aim to score points by throwing the ball so that it bounces in the square at the opposite end, but they must play through one of the gates before they can attempt to score. If possession is lost, they must play through the gate again. They are allowed to pass through either gate in either direction, but are not allowed to move with the ball in their hands.

Key skills

Progressions and alternatives:
1 Change the type of pass to practise different skills, such as a chest pass, overhead throw, bounce pass or underarm throw.
2 Teams must play through both gates before attempting to score.

session 58 switch tag

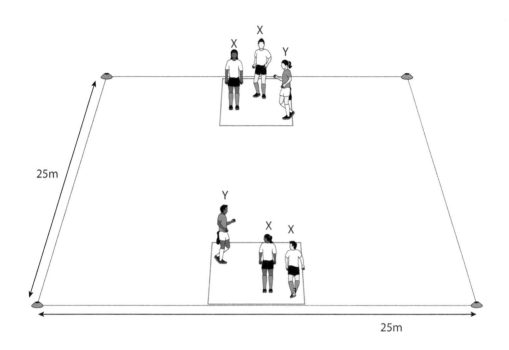

How to set up: Set out a 25 x 25m area, with two small squares at either end. Players are separated into two groups and stand in the squares.

What you need: Bibs, marker cones, balls.

How to play: One player from the group in each square holds a bib (Y) and tries to tag another player. If a player is tagged, they take the bib and become the 'tagger'. When the sports leader calls 'switch', the players race to swap squares. The last player to arrive at the other square becomes the next 'tagger'.

Key skills

Progressions and alternatives:
1 Add an extra tagger.
2 Change the type of movement between squares – backwards, sideways and skipping.
3 Give players different sports equipment to use as they move around, such as a football to dribble, a basketball to bounce, or a hockey stick and a ball to dribble.

session 59 shark bite

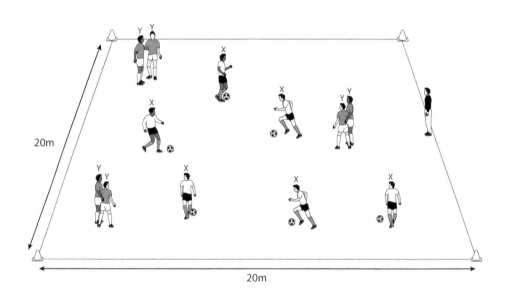

20m

20m

How to set up: Set out a 20 x 20m area. Y players act as defenders (sharks) and are joined together in pairs, either holding a bib between them or by linking arms. X players have a piece of sports equipment to use, depending on the theme of the session, such as a football to dribble, a basketball to bounce, or a hockey stick and a ball to dribble.

What you need: Bibs, traffic cones, sports equipment.

How to play: X players dribble their ball around the area avoiding the Y pairs (sharks). If one of the Y pairs steals their ball, they are out of the game.

Key skills

Progressions and alternatives:
1 If a player gets caught by a shark, they have to join on as an extra defender.
2 Give the sharks one ball between two, encouraging them to dribble the ball between them while trying to catch the X players.

session 60 protect the egg

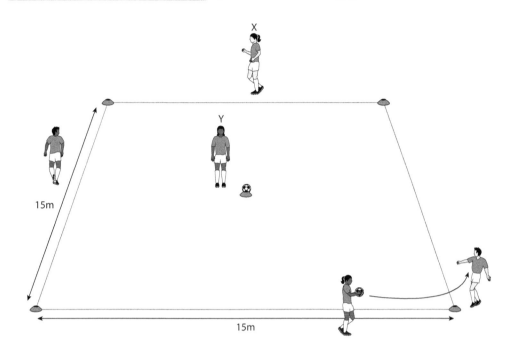

How to set up: Set out a 15 x 15m area, with a ball balanced on a traffic cone in the centre – the egg. Organise players into groups of five, with four players positioned on each side of the square (X) and one player in the middle area who protects the egg (Y). Repeat the area for a sufficient number of players.

What you need: Marker cones, traffic cone, balls.

How to play: The players pass the ball to each other around the outside of the area, aiming to create enough space to take a shot at the egg without the protector being able to block the shot. After a successful shot, swap the protector with a player on the outside.

Key skills

Progressions and alternatives:
1 Add a second egg protector.
2 Change the type of pass to practise different skills, such as a chest pass, overhead throw, bounce pass, or underarm throw.
3 Allow players to use their feet, or to use hockey sticks and a ball, to make it a sports-specific practice.

session 61 around the world

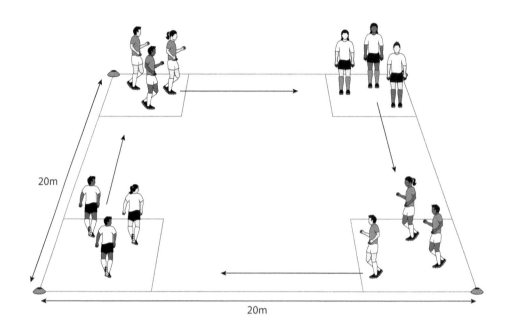

20m

20m

How to set up: Set out a 20 x 20m area with four 5 x 5m squares in each corner. Players are separated into teams of three and placed in each corner square. Each corner square is named after a place, country, city or landmark.

What you need: Bibs, marker cones.

How to play: Players are moving around in the corner squares, in and out of spaces without making contact with one another. As the sports leader shouts 'around the world', the players have to travel to the next square. Players move in a clockwise direction.

Key skills

Progressions and alternatives:
1 Introduce a 'tagger' in the space between the squares; as the players swap squares they now have to get past the tagger and into the next square. If a player is tagged, they become the tagger for the next round.
2 Give players different sports equipment to use as they move around in and between the corner squares, such as a football to dribble, a basketball to bounce, or a hockey stick and a ball to dribble.

session 62 bull's eye

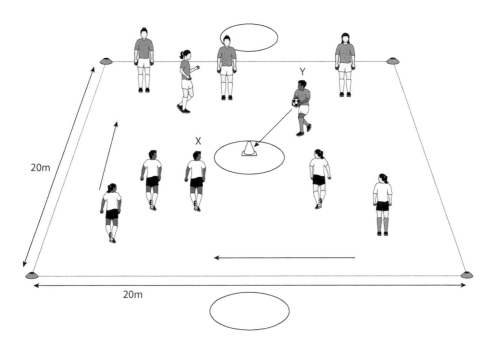

How to set up: Set out a 20 x 20m area with one hoop at each end and a hoop in the centre of the area. Place a traffic cone in the middle of the centre hoop. Arrange players into two small-sided teams (4 v 4 or 5 v 5).

What you need: Bibs, marker cones, traffic cones, hoops, ball.

How to play: Players attempt to score points for their team by throwing the ball and knocking down the central 'bull's-eye' cone. Players are not allowed to move with the ball in their hands, and if a player has two hands on the ball, no one is permitted to tackle them. After a goal is scored, play resumes from the end hoop. No player is allowed to enter the 'bull's-eye' area.

Key skills

>

Progressions and alternatives:
1 Change the location of the bull's-eye or add an extra bull's-eye in another part of the area, such as at the ends or the corners.
2 If players begin to crowd around the bull's-eye, enforce a rule where if a team wins possession, they must play out to a player standing in one, or either, of the end hoops before they can attack the bull's-eye in order to create space.
3 Change the size and shape of the ball.

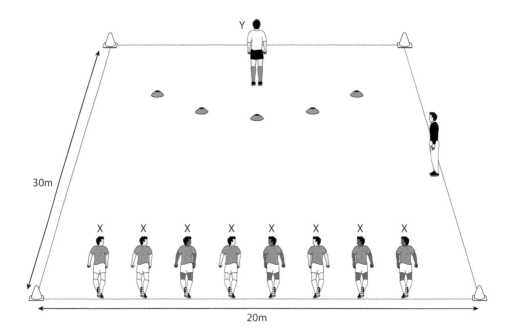

How to set up: Set out a 20 x 20m area. Each player (X) stands at the baseline. One player (Y) is standing at one end of the area and acts as the big bad wolf.

What you need: Bib, marker cones, traffic cones, balls.

How to play: The X players creep up to the big bad wolf (Y) and attempt to steal a cone. The big bad wolf (Y) has their eyes closed and stands so that they cannot see the X players approaching. The big bad wolf (Y) opens their eyes when they think they can hear the X players are near and tries to 'tag' as many players as possible. If the X players manage to steal a cone and make it back to the baseline they are 'safe'. Players who are tagged are now out and stand with the sports leader until all players have been tagged and play resumes with all players back in.

Key skills

Progressions and alternatives:
1 Have an additional big bad wolf.
2 Give players different sports equipment to use as they move around, such as a football to dribble, a basketball to bounce, or a hockey stick and a ball to dribble back to safety.

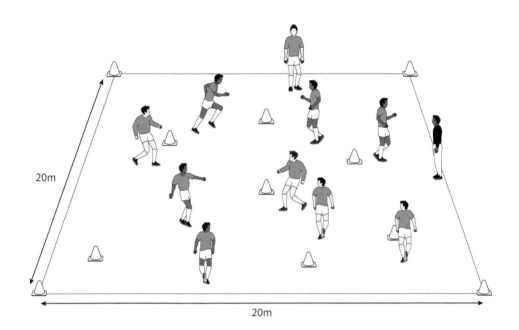

20m

20m

How to set up: Set out a 20 x 20m area. Scatter cones randomly around the area; there should be fewer cones than players.

What you need: Bibs, traffic cones.

How to play: Players move around the area. When the sports leader shouts 'cones', the players run and stand by the nearest cone. Any player who doesn't find a cone runs to another player and says 'excuse me please'. This player then has to move and find a new cone and the other player takes the first player's place. Any player without a cone after a 10-second countdown by the sports leader is out of the game or does a fun forfeit.

Key skills

Progressions and alternatives:
1 Change movement to skipping, hopping, and moving backwards or sideways.
2 Reduce countdown time to 5 seconds.
3 Reduce the number of cones, thereby increasing the number of players who go out of the game or do a fun forfeit.
4 Give players different sports equipment to use as they move around, such as a football to dribble, a basketball to bounce, or a hockey stick and a ball to dribble.

session 65 powerball

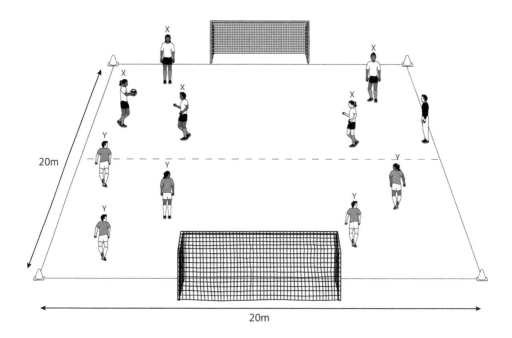

How to set up: Set out a 20 x 20m area, with a dividing line across the centre and a goal at each end. Select two teams – one on either side of the dividing line.

What you need: Bibs, marker cones, ball, large goal or traffic cones.

How to play: Each team tries to score by throwing the ball into the opposition's goal. Players must stay in their own half of the area.

Key skills

Progressions and alternatives:
1 Change the type of pass to practise different skills, such as overhead throw, underarm throw, or roll.
2 Introduce hockey sticks and a smaller ball so the players are using other sports equipment to try to score.

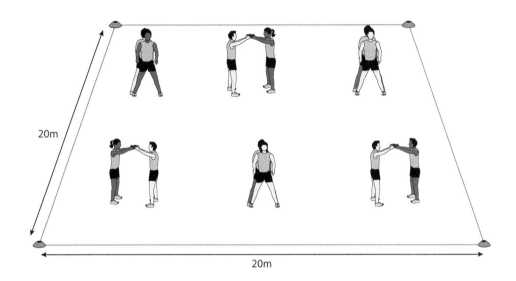

session 66 bridges and tunnels

20m

20m

How to set up: Set out a 20 x 20m area.

What you need: Bibs, marker cones.

How to play: Players move around inside the area. When the sports leader calls 'bridges', players find a partner and join up, face to face to make a bridge. When the sports leader calls 'tunnels', players find a partner and join up back to back with their legs apart to form a tunnel. The slowest pair is out of the game, with the last remaining pair the winners.

Key skills

Progressions and alternatives:
1 Change movements to skipping, hopping, and moving backwards or sideways.
2 Select two players to be taggers, who hold a bib each. As the sports leader calls 'bridges' or 'tunnels' the taggers attempt to tag the other players in the group before they are able to make a bridge or a tunnel. Any player who gets tagged now takes the bib and becomes a tagger.
3 As a progression from point 2, any player being chased by a tagger may now run under an existing bridge or tunnel. This breaks the bridge or tunnel and those two players are back in the game, are able to be tagged and must find a new partner to make a bridge or a tunnel with before getting tagged.

session 67 colour squares

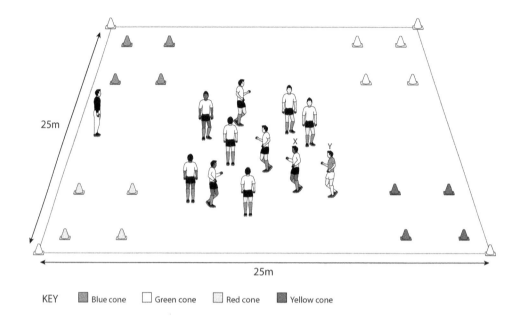

KEY ■ Blue cone □ Green cone □ Red cone ■ Yellow cone

How to set up: Set out a 25 x 25m area. Inside the area, mark out four different coloured smaller areas using traffic cones. The X players all stand inside the area, while a Y player (selected by the sports leader) stands at the edge of the area but closes or covers their eyes so that they cannot see.

What you need: Traffic cones, balls.

How to play: The sports leader gives the players inside the area a 5-second countdown. During this countdown the X players run around the area to find a square in which to stop. The sports leader asks the Y player to call out a colour, and anyone inside that coloured square is out of the game.

Key skills

Progressions and alternatives:
1 Change movements to each square (forwards, backwards, side to side).
2 Limit players to a 3-second countdown.
3 Give players different sports equipment to use as they move around, such as a football to dribble, a basketball to bounce, or a hockey stick and a ball to dribble.

session 68 the silent game

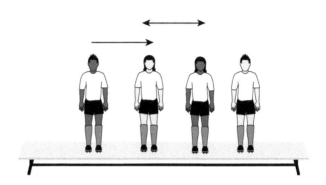

How to set up: Arrange players into small groups of four or five; they all stand on a bench, with one bench per team.

What you need: Benches.

How to play: Players stand on the benches and have to move to arrange themselves in the correct order depending on the subject, without talking to each other and without stepping off the bench. The sports leader decides the subject.

Key skills

Examples:
1 Age – oldest to youngest
2 Height – tallest to shortest
3 House numbers – highest to lowest
4 Shoe sizes – highest to lowest
5 Number of brothers and sisters – highest to lowest

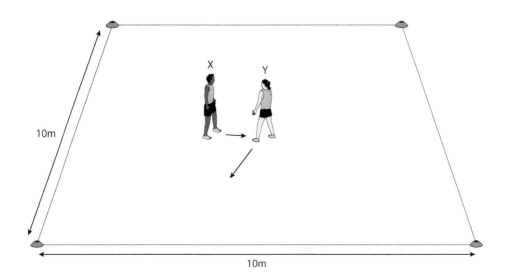

How to set up: Set out a 10 x 10m area. Players work in pairs. Repeat the area for the correct number of players.

What you need: Marker cones.

How to play: The two players face each other, with one player being the tagger. They must both stay facing each other at all times and must remain inside the area. The tagger tries to tag their partner on either knee, while the latter moves around trying to avoid being tagged. Once a tag is made, the players swap roles. Play for a specified length of time – whichever player is the tagger once the time is up loses.

Key skills

Progressions and alternatives:
1 Make the area bigger to make it harder for the tagger.
2 Make the area smaller to make it easier for the tagger.

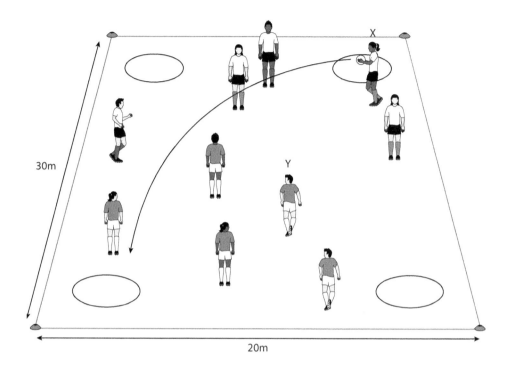

How to set up: Set out a 20 x 30m area with two hoops at each end, one in each corner. Organise the players into two teams, with each team attacking opposite ends.

What you need: Bibs, marker cones, four hoops, balls.

How to play: Players attempt to score a point for their team by throwing the ball so that it bounces inside one of the hoops, without hitting the edge of the hoop. All players are permitted to move around, but may not step into the hoops at any point. Players are not allowed to move with the ball in their hands.

Key skills

Progressions and alternatives:
1 Teams to attack hoops that are diagonally across from each other, making the game multi-directional.
2 Limit players to a specific type of pass, such as a bounce pass, or only an underarm or overarm throw.
3 Change the size and/or shape of the balls.

session 71 desert island discs

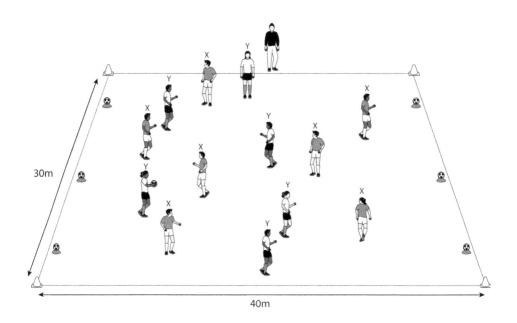

30m

40m

How to set up: Set out a 20 x 30m area. Place three balls balanced on cones across both sidelines, and arrange the group into small-sided teams (5 v 5 or 4 v 4).

What you need: Bibs, marker cones, balls.

How to play: Players aim to score points by throwing the ball to knock the three balls on the sideline off the cones. The other team tries to intercept the ball. Players are not allowed to move with the ball in their hands, and the first team to knock down the three balls at the other end of the area wins.

Key skills

Progressions and alternatives:
1 Limit players to a specific type of pass, such as a bounce pass, or only an underarm or overarm throw.
2 Change the size and/or shape of the ball.
3 Increase the number of target balls on the baselines.

session 72 hop it!

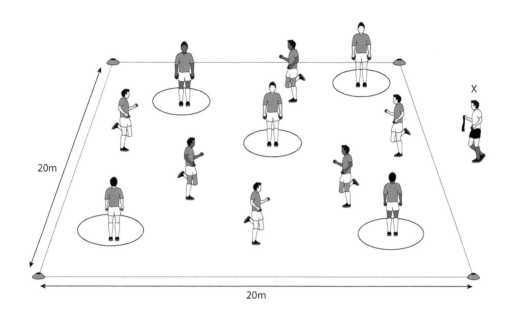

How to set up: Set out a 20 x 20m area, with five hoops scattered randomly around it.

What you need: Bibs, marker cones, hoops.

How to play: Select one player to be the tagger (X) who holds a bib in their hand and waits outside the area. All other players move around the area. When the sports leader calls out 'hop it', the tagger enters the game and tries to tag as many players as possible. The players inside the area are now only allowed to hop around, but are safe if they are standing in a hoop – although players may only stand inside any hoop for 3 seconds at a time. Any tagged player is out of the game, with the last remaining player being the winner.

Key skills

Progressions and alternatives:

1 Add more hoops to make it harder for the tagger; or remove hoops to make it harder for the players.
2 Increase or decrease the amount of time allowed in any hoop.
3 Change movements to skipping or jumping.

How to set up: Set out five different-colour cones in a line, 10m away from two central traffic cones which are set at staggered distances. Organise players into pairs.

What you need: Traffic cones.

How to play: One player from each pair stands with their hand on a traffic cone. As the sports leader calls a colour, the two players race to touch the cone of that colour, then back to their opponent's cone. The first player back scores a point, and the first player to 5 points wins.

Key skills

Progressions and alternatives:
1 Increase the distance between the coloured cones and the traffic cones.
2 The sports leader calls more than one colour or a set combination of colours.

How to set up: Set out a circle with marker cones, and position one player (Y) in the middle with all the other players (X) on the outside.

What you need: Marker cones, soft balls.

How to play: The players around the edge of the circle throw the ball, aiming to hit the player in the middle below the waist. Each time the player is hit, the thrower scores a point; swap turns after 30 seconds and, once all the players have had a turn in the middle, the player with the highest score is declared the winner.

Key skills

Progressions and alternatives:
1 Make the circle bigger or smaller.
2 Change the size of the ball.
3 Add more balls.
4 Players work in pairs in the centre.

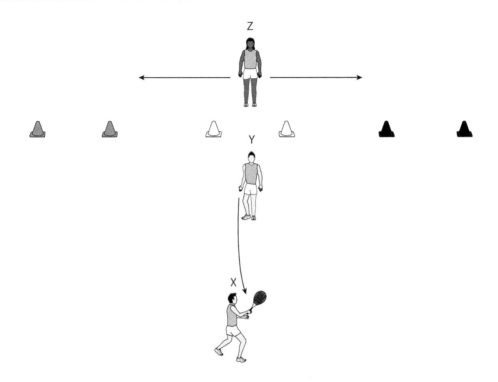

session 75 target practice

How to set up: Set our three mini goals or gates – each one needs to be a different colour. Organise players into groups of three and give a piece of sports equipment (such as a tennis racket, a cricket bat or a hockey stick) to one player (X) who acts as the batter, and a ball to one player (Y), who acts as the server. The third player (Z) acts as a fielder and stands behind the mini goals. Repeat the area for the correct number of players.

What you need: Traffic cones, sports equipment, balls.

How to play: The bowler throws the ball and calls a colour; the batter has to try to use the equipment to hit the ball into that colour mini goal or gate to score a point. Give each player ten turns in each role; whichever player has the most points is the winner.

Key skills

Progressions and alternatives:
1 Allow the fielder to stand in front of, and defend, the mini goals or gates.
2 Only allow the bowler and the batter to use their weaker hand or arm.
3 Make the mini goals or gates larger or smaller.

session 76 messy room

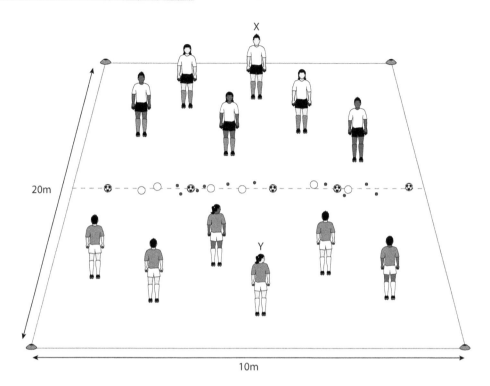

X

20m

Y

10m

How to set up: Set out a 10 x 20m area with a central dividing line across the middle. Organise players into two teams who stay in their own half at all times, and scatter a range of balls, quoits, bean bags and other sports equipment across the central line.

What you need: Marker cones, balls, quoits, bean bags.

How to play: When the sports leader calls 'go', both teams race from their end-line to collect the equipment from the middle, and then have to throw it into the other team's half of the area. Play for 30 seconds; whichever team has the least amount of toys (objects) in their room (area) is the winner.

Key skills

Progressions and alternatives:

1 Limit players to a specific type of throw – such as overarm, underarm or overhead throw.
2 Only allow players to throw with their weaker arm.

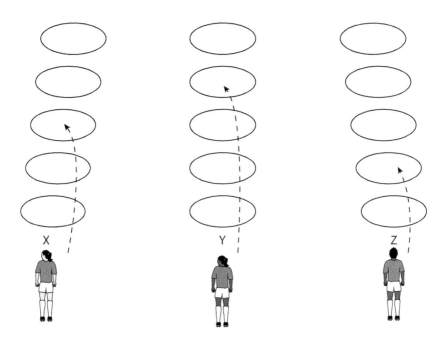

How to set up: Organise players into three teams who stand at the start point with five hoops set out in front of each team, at increasing distances. Each team needs five bean bags.

What you need: Marker cones, bean bags, hoops.

How to play: When the sports leader shouts 'go', the teams race to fill their hoops by throwing the bean bags to land and stay inside of them. Players take it in turns in their teams, and the first team to fill all five of their hoops wins.

Key skills

Progressions and alternatives:
1 Only allow players to throw with their weaker arm.
2 Only allow players to throw at the hoops in the order of distance, closest one first, and finishing up with the furthest hoop.
3 Increase the distances of the hoops.

How to set up: Organise two players into pairs who stand facing each other. One player holds two bean bags. Repeat the area for the correct number of players.

What you need: Bean bags.

How to play: Two players stand facing each other; one stands holding the bean bags out at shoulder height with the other player standing in front of them, and then drops one of the bean bags. The player holding the bean bags may drop a bean bag at any time so their opponent needs to be ready to react and try to catch it before it hits the ground. If it hits the ground, the player who was holding the bean bag scores a point, but if the bean bag is caught, the player catching it scores a point. The first player to 5 points wins; then swap roles.

Key skills

Progressions and alternatives:
1 Hold the bean bags higher (above the head) to give the catcher an advantage.
2 Hold the bean bags lower (waist height) to give the holder of it an advantage.
3 Change bean bags for heavier or lighter objects.

session 79 tennis ball relay

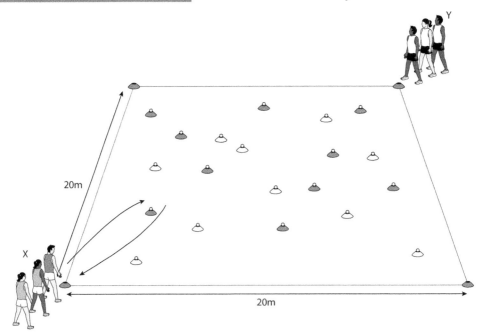

How to set up: Set out a 20 x 20m area with ten red cones and ten blue cones scattered around the area. Balance a tennis ball on each of the cones and organise the players into two teams, one red team (X) and one blue team (Y), with each team stationed in opposite corners of the area.

What you need: Traffic cones, marker cones, tennis balls (or any type of small ball), a plastic box, bucket or container.

How to play: Players race one per team at a time to collect a tennis ball from on top of a cone and to bring the balls back to their team. The players in the red team only collect the balls on the red cones, and the players in the blue team only collect the balls on the blue cones. Once a ball is collected it must be thrown back to the team and caught. If the ball is dropped, it is placed back on top of the cone, and the next player goes. The first team to have collected, thrown and caught all of their ten tennis balls is the winner.

Key skills

Progressions and alternatives:
1 Any throw may only be caught with one hand.
2 Only allow a bounce pass – so the ball has to bounce once in between the thrower and the catcher.
3 Add a box, bucket or container to throw the tennis balls into once collected, requiring a more accurate throw.

session 80 safety cone

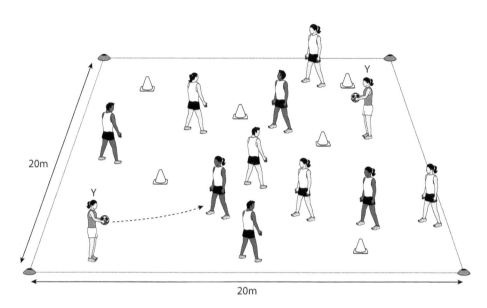

How to set up: Set out a 20 x 20m area, with larger safety cones (traffic cones) scattered around the inside. Two players hold a soft ball each (Y) all players are in the area.

What you need: Marker cones, traffic cones, soft balls.

How to play: The player holding the ball aims to hit the other players below the knee by rolling the ball along the floor. Any player hit by the ball is eliminated, but if a player is standing with a hand on any one of the safety cones they are safe and cannot be hit by the ball. All players may move around the area, but may only stand by a safety cone for 5 seconds at a time. The sports leader will need to remove the safety cones one by one as the game progresses in order to finish the game with one remaining winner.

Key skills

Progressions and alternatives:
1 Start the game with more players holding a ball.
2 Reduce the amount of time any player may stand by a safety cone.
3 Once a player is eliminated they pick up a ball and join in, trying to eliminate other players.

How to set up: Organise players to stand in a circle, with one player standing in the middle.

What you need: Ball.

How to play: The players in the circle pass the ball (the bomb) around in a clockwise direction while the player in the middle counts down from 20. Once the countdown gets to 10 seconds, it becomes silent. Whoever is holding the bomb when the countdown gets to zero is out, and the last remaining player is the winner.

Key skills

Progressions and alternatives:
1 Players may throw the ball to any other player in the circle.
2 Increase/decrease the countdown.
3 The whole of the countdown is silent.

session 82 bounce ball

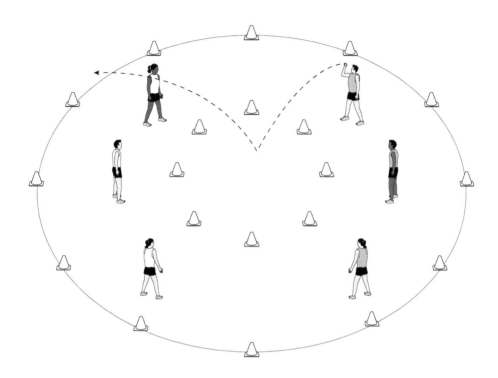

How to set up: Set out a large circle 20m wide, with a smaller circle – 5m wide – in the middle. Organise players into two teams of three or four, with one team on each side of the circle.

What you need: Bibs, traffic cones, bouncy balls.

How to play: Players aim to score points by throwing the ball into the smaller circle so that it bounces, then lands, outside the larger circle. If they are successful, they get 2 points. If the throw is blocked, then no points are scored, but if the ball is caught by the other team before it bounces outside the larger circle, that team gets 1 point. The first team to 10 points wins.

Key skills

Progressions and alternatives:
1 Change the size and/or shape of the ball.
2 Allow players to be spread around the circle, so they can throw from multiple angles.
3 Increase/decrease the number of players on each team to create more/less space and scoring opportunities.

session 83 buckets

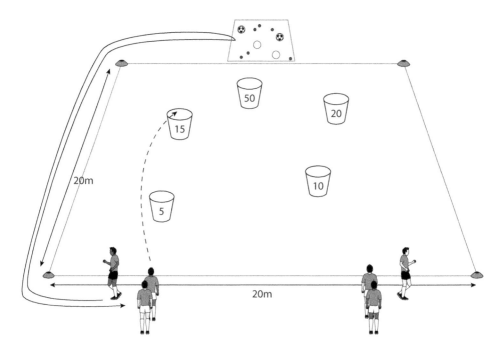

How to set up: Set out a 20 x 20m area with five buckets, bins, crates (or whatever you can find) scattered randomly around the area. Label each bucket with a points value – 5, 10, 15, 20 and 50. Create a 5 x 5m 'ball pit' at the back of the area and fill it with balls (various sizes and shapes) and bean bags. Organise players into two teams.

What you need: Buckets, balls, sports equipment.

How to play: When the sports leader shouts 'go', the first player in each team races around the outside of the area to collect a ball from the 'ball pit', then back to the start point. The player then attempts to throw the ball into the bucket of their choice to score points. Whichever bucket the ball lands in, the team scores that amount of points. The first team to score 100 points wins.

Key skills

Progressions and alternatives:

1 Limit players to a specific type of throw – such as an overarm, underarm or overhead throw.
2 The ball has to bounce at least once before it goes in the bucket to score points.
3 Give players different sports equipment to use as they aim for the buckets, such as a tennis racket or a cricket bat.

octopus

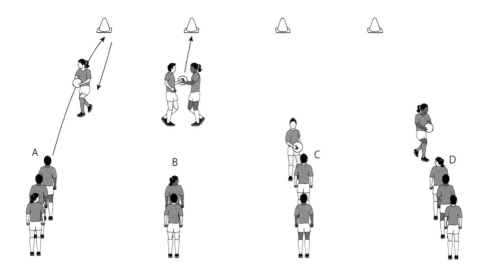

How to set up: Arrange four teams into a relay-type race with one ball per team and set out one cone in front of each team. The distance will depend on the age of the players.

What you need: Traffic cones, balls.

How to play: When the sports leader says 'go', the first player in each team runs to the cone with the ball in both hands and then returns to their team as fast as they can. When they get back to the start point, they collect the next person in their team. The two players now run together, both holding the ball so that there are now four hands on the ball. Each time they return to the start point they collect another player to join in, and the first team to complete the race with their whole team holding the ball wins.

Key skills

Progressions and alternatives:
1 Use a beach ball or a balloon for younger players, and a tennis ball for older players.
2 Introduce staggered relay points to race to.

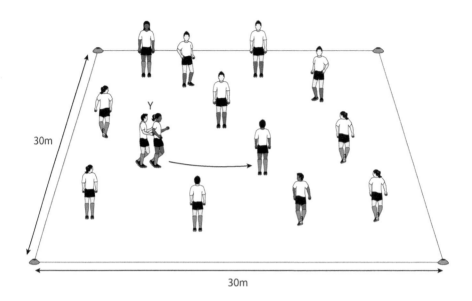

How to set up: Set out a 30 x 30m area, with all players standing inside the square.

What you need: Marker cones.

How to play: Select one player to be the monster (Y), who chases the other players around the area. When the monster tags another player, that player joins on with the monster to become a two-headed monster and they have to work together to try to catch another player in order to become a three-headed monster. Play continues until you have one player remaining who is the winner.

Key skills

Progressions and alternatives:
1 Start with two monsters – whichever monster ends the game with the most heads wins.
2 Make the area smaller.

session 86 king's corner

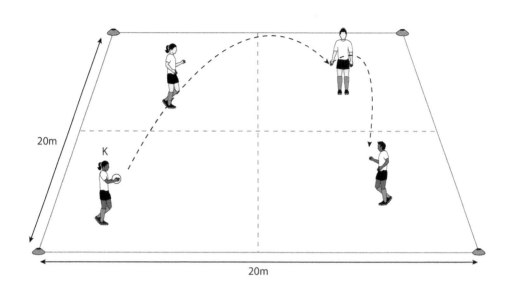

How to set up: Set out a 20 x 20m area which is then divided into four equal 5 x 5m quarters, with one square marked as the 'kings corner' (K). Organise players into groups of four, with one player in each quarter and one waiting by the side. Repeat the area for a sufficient number of players.

What you need: Marker cones, large bouncy ball.

How to play: Each player plays as an individual against the other three players. The game is played to a time limit (3 or 4 minutes), with the aim of the game to be the player in the king's corner once the time limit expires. The king starts with the ball and bounces it in another square. The player in that square has to return the ball to any other player in the square by hitting it with the palm of their hand. The ball must bounce inside the area, and each player must try to prevent the ball from bouncing twice in their area. Once a point is won or a mistake is made, the players move around in a clockwise direction – so if a player wins a serve, they move closer to, or take the place of, the king, but if they make a mistake, they move further away.

Key skills

Progressions and alternatives:
1 Decrease or increase the amount of playing time.
2 Change the size of the ball.
3 Introduce tennis rackets and balls to make this game sports-specific.

session 87 doctor, doctor

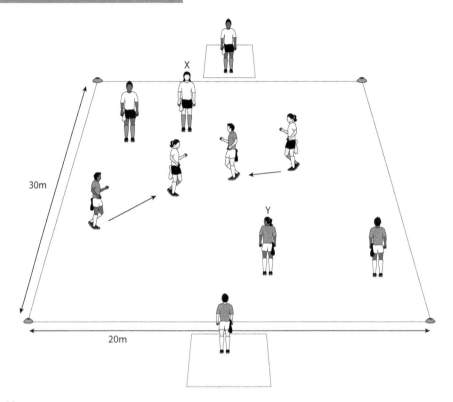

How to set up: Mark out a 20 x 30m area with a smaller square at each end. Organise the players into two even teams, with one player from each team (the doctor) stationed in one of the smaller squares. All players need a rugby tag or a bib hanging from the waistband of their trousers or shorts.

What you need: Bibs, marker cones.

How to play: The players in the area have to chase the players on the opposing team and try to pull out their bib/tag. If a player is caught, they have to go down on one knee and are out of the game, but if they call their doctor to come and give them a high five, they are back in. To win the game you need to catch the other team's doctor while they are outside of their square, but if they are in their square, they are safe.

Key skills

Progressions and alternatives:

1 Allow each team to have two doctors.
2 Introduce sports equipment such as basketballs, footballs, or hockey balls and sticks to dribble around in order to make it sports-specific.

session 88 catch a fish

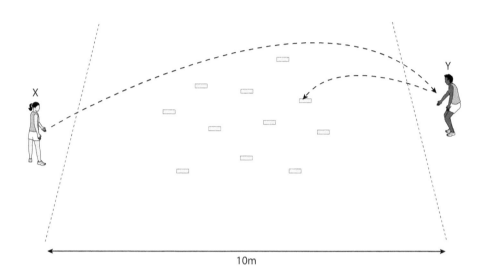

X

Y

10m

How to set up: Organise players into pairs who stand opposite each other, behind lines 10m apart. Place an odd number of bean bags on the floor in the gap between the two players and give one of the players a tennis ball. Repeat the area for the correct number of players.

What you need: Marker cones, bean bags, tennis balls.

How to play: Players throw the ball to each other underarm across the 'river' (the gap). If a player catches a ball successfully (without dropping it), they may reach into the river and catch a 'fish' (bean bag) – but without stepping into the river. Whichever player catches the most fish is the winner.

Key skills

Progressions and alternatives:
1 Increase or decrease the gap between the players.
2 Increase or decrease the size of the ball used.
3 Only allow players to throw and catch using one hand.

session 89 balloon volleyball

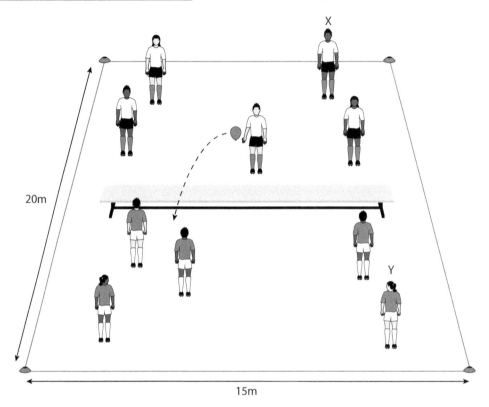

X

20m

15m

How to set up: Set out a 15 x 20m area with a bench (or two) placed across the middle, separating the two halves of the area. Organise the players into two teams and station them on either side of the area.

What you need: Marker cones, benches, balloons.

How to play: This game is the same as volleyball, but is played with a balloon instead of a ball. The players have to hit the ball to the other side of the area using their hands, and prevent the balloon from hitting the floor on their side. If the balloon hits the floor, the other team get a point; the first team to get to 10 points wins.

Key skills

Progressions and alternatives:
1 Play the game with all players sitting down.
2 Restrict the amount of touches of the balloon per side.
3 Swap the balloon for an actual volleyball or a larger, light ball.

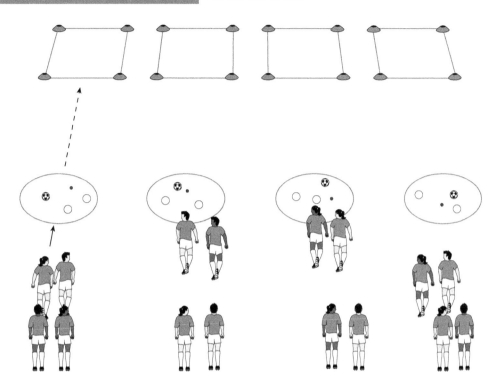

session 90 travel ball

How to set up: Organise players into groups of four at a start point, with a small square at the other side of the area, 15–20m away. Place a hoop in the middle of the start and finish points with four assorted sizes and shapes of balls, bean bags and other items in it. Repeat for the correct number of players.

What you need: Marker cones, assortment of balls, hoops.

How to play: Working in pairs, the players run from the start point to collect a ball from the hoop and transport it to the end square – without using their hands! If a ball is dropped on the way to the square, it is placed back in the hoop and the next pair in that team take their turn. The first team to successfully transport their four items from the hoop to the finish point wins.

Key skills

Progressions and alternatives:
1 Add more items to the hoop.
2 Players race one at a time.
3 Increase the distance between the hoop and the finish point.

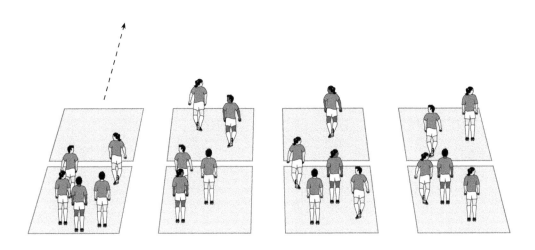

How to set up: Organise players into groups of four or five, and give each group two gym mats to stand on. Start each team at one end of the area. This game is best suited to an indoor hall space.

What you need: Gym mats.

How to play: All teams start at one end of the hall. The aim of the game is to get to the other end without any team member touching the floor. If any team member steps off the mat and touches the floor, they have to start again, and the first team to make it to the other end wins.

Key skills

Progressions and alternatives:

1 Have one or two players at the side of the area rolling balls across, trying to hit the players on the mats. If a player is hit the whole team goes back to the start.
2 Add some obstacles to the area, such as benches.
3 Give the players on the mats a tennis ball to transport from one end to the other, but they must not touch the tennis ball with their hands.

session 92 crabtastic

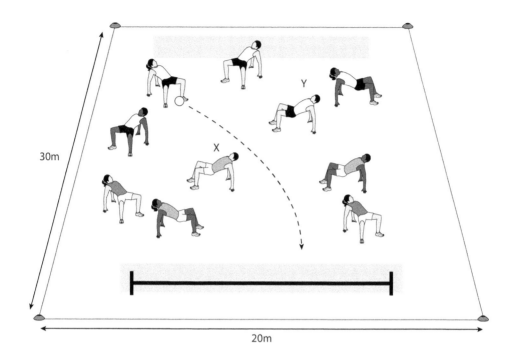

30m

20m

How to set up: Set out a 20 x 30m area with a bench at each end placed on its side. Organise the players into two teams.

What you need: Bibs, marker cones, benches, ball.

How to play: Each team aims to score a point by throwing the ball to hit the face of the other team's bench. Players may not move when in possession of the ball and may not tackle any other player when in possession. All players must also be in the 'crab' position at all times – facing upwards but with both hands and feet on the floor.

Key skills

Progressions and alternatives:
1 Every player on the team must touch the ball before a goal can be scored.
2 A minimum of five passes must be made before a goal can be scored.
3 Change the size or shape of the ball.

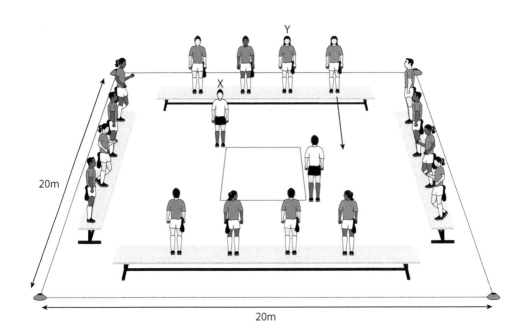

How to set up: Set out a 20 x 20m area with a bench on each side. Mark out a 5 x 5m 'prison' in the middle of the area and give each player a bib to tuck into the waistband of their trousers or shorts, hanging down like a tail – except for two players who act as the prison guards. Organise players into four teams and station them on one bench per team.

What you need: Bibs, marker cones, benches.

How to play: Each team takes it in turns to escape from prison, by running around inside the area without getting caught by the prison guards for an allocated amount of time (20 seconds). If any player is caught (bib pulled out), they have to stand in the prison in the middle of the area. No player may go in the prison during the game unless they have been caught. Once the time elapses, the remaining uncaught players return to their bench, then another team takes their turn. Whichever team has the most players on their bench at the end of the game is the winner.

Key skills

Progressions and alternatives:
1 Increase/decrease the number of prison guards to make it harder/easier.
2 Increase/decrease the amount of prison break time to make it harder/easier.
3 Play with two teams at a time head to head.

session 94 cone colour pairs

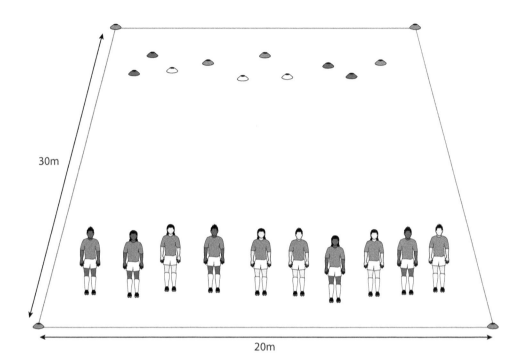

30m

20m

How to set up: Set out a 20 x 30m area and place a number of different-colour cones at the end of the area. Get the players to stand at the other end with their backs to the cones so that they can't see them.

What you need: Marker cones, sports equipment.

How to play: The sports leader gives each player a cone that corresponds to a colour at the other end of the area – you need to make sure you have the same colours at the other end as you are giving to the players, and the correct amount. When the sports leader calls 'go', the players turn and race to find the same colour cone (the pair) as they have been given. The first player to do this wins a point. Repeat the game; the first player to reach 10 points wins.

Key skills

Progressions and alternatives:
1 Ask the player to stand with their eyes closed and place the cone on the floor in front of them so that they have to first spot the colour, then react to find the pair.
2 Give players different sports equipment to use as they race, such as a tennis ball and racket, a football or basketball.

session 95 centipede tag

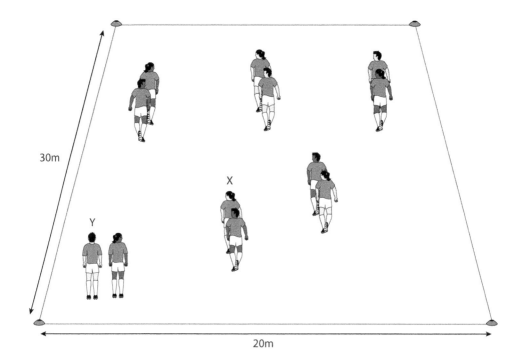

How to set up: Set out a 20 x 20m area. Organise players into pairs.

What you need: Marker cones.

How to play: Choose one pair to be the taggers (Y) who chase the other pairs around the area. If a pair are caught and tagged, they are frozen. If another pair join up with the frozen pair, they become unfrozen, but they are now joined up as a team of four, and if they unfreeze another pair, they become a team of six and so on. Play for a minute and whichever group has the highest number of players without being frozen wins.

Key skills

Progressions and alternatives:
1 Players start the game as individuals, not pairs.
2 Reduce or increase the time limit.
3 Give the taggers a soft ball to throw at the other players in order to tag them; if they get hit, they are frozen.

stoppers, starters and activators

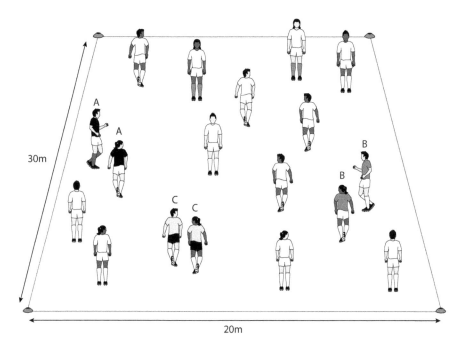

How to set up: Mark out a 20 x 20m area. Select two players to be 'stoppers' (A) and give them blue bibs; two players to be 'activators' (B) and give them red bibs; and two players to be 'starters' (C) and give them yellow bibs. (Colours of bibs aren't important, provided you have two of each colour.) The rest of the players are in the area.

What you need: Bibs, marker cones, balls.

How to play: The stoppers and activators move around in the area, trying to tag the rest of the group. If a player is tagged by a stopper, they are frozen and have to stand still like a statue. If a player is tagged by an activator, they have to perform an action, such as hopping/jogging on the spot, star jumps or dancing. The action needs to be predetermined before the start of the game. These players are 'frozen' or activated until tagged by the starters, and then they may return to the game. Play for 30 seconds, then change the players around.

Key skills

Progressions and alternatives:

1 Increase the number of stoppers, starters and activators.
2 Increase the time limit.
3 Give the stoppers and activators soft balls to hit the other players with instead of tagging them.

session 97 speed snatch

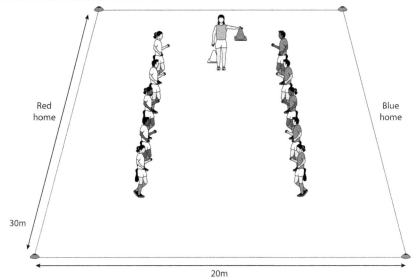

Red home

Blue home

30m

20m

How to set up: Set out a 20 x 30m area with two parallel lines 10m apart in the centre of the area. Divide the players into two teams and station the teams on parallel lines. Give each player a bib to tuck into the waistband of their shorts, to hang down like a tail. Assign one team to be the red team (X) and the other to be the blue team (Y).

What you need: Bibs, marker cones, traffic cones.

How to play: The sports leader stands in front of the two teams on the parallel lines and holds two cones behind their back, one red and one blue. They then hold up either the red or blue cone – at their discretion. If they hold up the blue cone, the blue team have to race to get to their home line at the edge of the area, while the red team chase them and try to pull their tails out before they get home, and vice versa. If a tail is pulled out by a player on the chasing team, 1 point is gained for their team, but if a player from the running team makes it back to their home line, they get 1 point for their team. The team with the most points after an allocated time period, or after an equal amount of turns, wins.

Key skills

Progressions and alternatives:
1 Have the players perform exercises while standing on the parallel lines, such as star jumps, jogging on the spot, or hopping.
2 Give the players a piece of sports equipment to use while they are trying to get home, such as a football or basketball to dribble.
3 Allow players to move around the whole area, without a home area. Give a 10-second countdown and see how many players manage to keep their tails.

session 98 corner ball

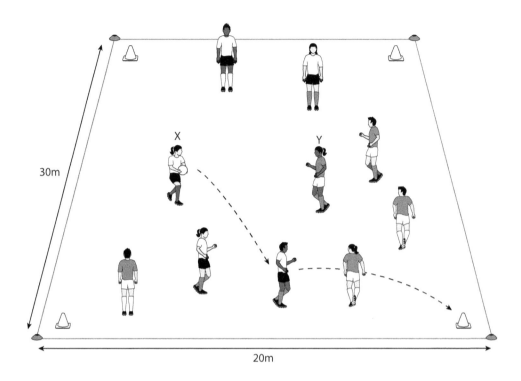

30m

20m

How to set up: Set out a 20 x 30m area with a traffic cone standing in each corner. Organise the players into two teams of no more than 6 v 6.

What you need: Bibs, marker cones, traffic cones, ball.

How to play: The teams attempt to score points by throwing the ball and knocking down the traffic cones in the corners of the area, but can only attack the two cones at opposite corners of the area. Players may not move with the ball in their hands, and opposing players are not permitted to tackle or knock the ball out of a player's hand, only to intercept passes.

Key skills

Progressions and alternatives:
1 Only allow teams to attack the two cones at opposite ends.
2 Limit players to a specific type of pass, such as a bounce pass, or only an underarm or overarm throw.
3 Change the size and shape of the ball.

session 99 ball point

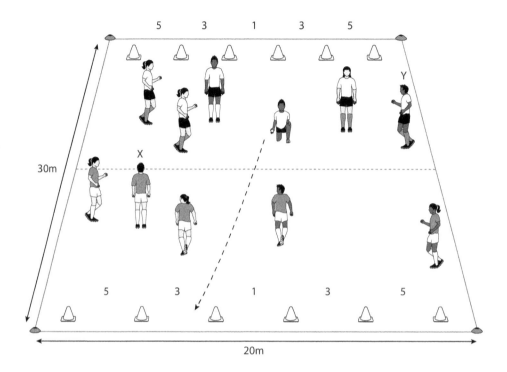

How to set up: Set out a 20 x 30m area with a central line dividing the area into two halves. Place traffic cones along each of the baselines, creating five small goals, which are each given a points value. Organise players into two teams and position one team in each of the halves of the area.

What you need: Bibs, marker cones, traffic cones, tennis balls.

How to play: Each team aims to score points by rolling the tennis ball along the floor so that it passes through one of the small goals on the opponent's baseline. For a successful roll, the team score the number of points allocated to that goal. All players must stay in their own half and may try to stop the ball going into the small goals by using only their feet. Set a target number of points. The first team to reach the target wins.

Key skills

Progressions and alternatives:
1 Players may use any part of their bodies to stop the ball, except for their feet.
2 Give each player a hockey stick to try to hit the ball through the small goals, to make it more sports-specific.

session 100 colour scramble

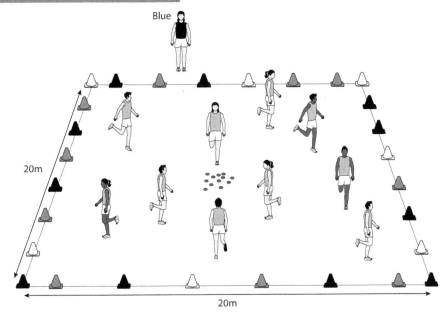

Blue

20m

20m

How to set up: Set out a 20 x 20m area with many different-colour cones. Scatter some bean bags on the floor in the centre of the area; there needs to be one less bean bag than the total number of players.

What you need: Traffic cones, bean bags, balls.

How to play: Players move around the area performing different types of movements, such as jogging, hopping or skipping. The sports leader then calls out a colour, and the players have to sprint to the outside of the area to touch a cone of that colour, then race to the middle of the area a pick up a bean bag. The player who isn't quick enough to get a bean bag is out of the game, or has to do a fun forfeit such as ten star jumps. Keep removing the bean bags and play until you have one remaining winner.

Key skills

Progressions and alternatives:
1 Replace the bean bags with balls of different sizes or shapes – one ball less than the total number of players.
2 Allow players to move around with the balls, such as dribbling basketballs with hands, or dribbling footballs with feet. When a colour is called, the players leave their ball and touch the cone of that colour, and then return to pick up a different ball.
3 The one player without a ball may steal a ball from another player if they lose control of their ball while moving around the area.

session 101 off ground tag

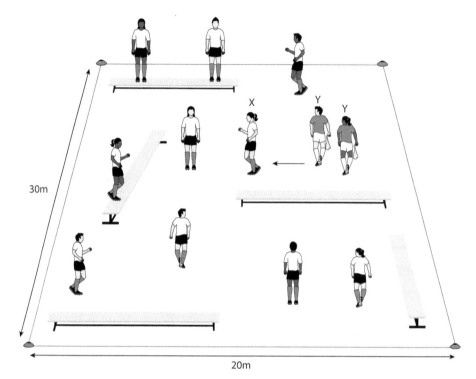

30m

20m

How to set up: Set out a 20 x 30m area with benches placed in various positions around it. This game works best when played in an inside space. Choose two players from the group to be taggers (Y), who hold a bib each.

What you need: Bibs, marker cones, benches.

How to play: The taggers have to try to catch the other players who are moving around the area, trying not to get tagged. If any player is standing on the bench – i.e. off the ground – they are safe and may not be tagged, but they may only be on any bench for three seconds at a time. If a player is moving between benches and is in contact with the ground (X), they may be tagged; that player is then out of the game. The last remaining player wins.

Key skills

Progressions and alternatives:

1 Increase/decrease the amount of time any player can spend on the benches.
2 Change the movement of the players between the benches to skipping or hopping.
3 Increase the amount of taggers.
4 Any player who is tagged takes the bib and becomes the tagger.